English

P9-CCV-460

p. 10   postulates

About the USA Group Foundation

The purpose of the USA Group Foundation is to carry out the research and philanthropic goals of USA Group, Inc., with special emphasis on improving higher education. Specifically, the Foundation supports original and sponsored research, and sponsors selected educational activities. The Foundation also supports educational and civic nonprofit endeavors primarily in the communities where USA Group employees live and work.

The Foundation concentrates its resources in three broad areas: research, program support, and philanthropy. Throughout all its efforts, the Foundation is especially interested in partnering with other foundations, corporations, research institutes, educational associations, and donors.

Additional information about the USA Group Foundation may be obtained by writing the Foundation at P.O. Box 7039, Indianapolis, Indiana 46207-7039, or visiting the website at www.usagroup.com.

Prioritizing Academic Programs and Services

Robert C. Dickeson

Foreword by Stanley O. Ikenberry

Prioritizing Academic Programs and Services

Reallocating Resources to Achieve Strategic Balance

Published in Association
with the USA Group Foundation

Jossey-Bass Publishers • San Francisco

Jossey-Bass books and products are available through most bookstores. To contact Jossey-Bass directly, call (888) 378-2537, fax to (800) 605-2665, or visit our website at www.josseybass.com.

Substantial discounts on bulk quantities of Jossey-Bass books are available to corporations, professional associations, and other organizations. For details and discount information, contact the special sales department at Jossey-Bass.

Epigraph in Chapter Eight from Glen, P. *It's Not My Department! How America Can Return to Excellence—Giving and Receiving Quality Service*. Copyright © by Peter Glen. Used by permission of William Morrow & Co., Inc.

Epigraph in Chapter Nine by F. Scott Fitzgerald, from *The Crack-Up*. Copyright © 1945 by New Directions Publishing Corp. Reprinted by permission of New Directions Publishing Corp.

Manufactured in the United States of America on Lyons Falls Turin Book. This paper is acid-free and 100 percent totally chlorine-free.

Library of Congress Cataloging-in-Publication Data

Dickeson, Robert C.
    Prioritizing academic programs and services : reallocating resources to achieve strategic balance / Robert C. Dickeson ; foreword by Stanley O. Ikenberry. — 1st ed.
        p.   cm. — (Jossey Bass higher and adult education series)
    "Published in Association with the USA Group Foundation."
    Includes bibliographical references and index.
    ISBN 0-7879-4816-0 (cloth : acid-free paper)
    1. Universities and colleges—United States—Administration. 2. Educational leadership—United States. 3. Educational change—United States. 4. Universities and colleges—United States—Sociological aspects. 5. Universities and colleges—United States—Administration—Case studies. 6. Educational change—United States—Case studies. 7. Educational leadership—United States—Case studies. 8. Universities and colleges—United States—Sociological aspects—Case studies. 9. n-us I. Title. II. Series.
    LB2341 .D523 1999
    378.73—dc21   98-40254

FIRST EDITION
HB Printing   10 9 8 7 6 5 4 3 2

The Jossey-Bass

Higher and Adult Education Series

Contents

Foreword

The crucial challenge facing American higher education today is that of defining a sense of self. Each of the thirty-six hundred or so colleges and universities in the United States has a unique heritage. Each vision, each purpose, each institutional character is distinctive. The special strengths and the comparative advantages of the campuses differ, one from another. Defining a sense of self is a complex task.

Bob Dickeson offers a sound conceptual framework and a set of processes for clarifying institutional purpose and setting academic priorities. There is no job more difficult—or more important. When priorities are on the table, academic lives and careers are at risk. Trustees face the challenge of weighing priorities at virtually every meeting and, more intensely, in times of crisis. Faculty members help shape the academic ethos and bring it to life. Alumni, legislators, governors, the media, campus communities, special interest groups—all play a role in shaping or ignoring academic program priorities.

Ultimately, the success of the academic presidency can be measured by how creatively presidents and other academic leaders engage the academic community in choosing among the ubiquitous and competing demands for financial and physical resources. In most instances, all demands and all programs are important. But in the end, some are crucial; if ignored, they may well imperil the institution, its quality, its character, and in some instances, its very survival. The future of American higher education—our quality and our capacity to serve society and fulfill our promise—rests in no small part on stronger presidential-trustee-faculty leadership in clarifying our sense of purpose and the priorities that follow.

Why does setting academic priorities matter? If resources to fund academic progress were inexhaustible, then perhaps setting priorities might be less important. However, although American higher education, unlike its counterpart institutions in almost every other nation, is fortunate to be able to draw on multiple sources of financial support—student tuition and fees, endowment earnings, direct and indirect support from federal and state governments, corporate support, and gifts from alumni and friends— in reality each of these sources has an ultimate limit, and many campuses are presently testing those limits. Even at the strongest, best-supported campuses, leaders face the struggle of maintaining quality, staying at the cutting edge, and responding to demands for additional resources. Indeed, it is at the nation's greatest centers of academic talent and strength that the struggle over academic priorities can be most intense. Creative ideas, compelling opportunities, and talented people combine to intensify the pressure to gain some sense of priorities.

The relationship between academic quality and financial resources has always been apparent; an institution's financial health is crucial to its academic quality. The paradigm has shifted, however, or at least it has expanded, to recognize that academic quality also is linked to purposeful and efficient *utilization* of resources. Monies wasted or underutilized mean fewer dollars for the academic priorities of greatest urgency. Using financial resources in purposeful, efficient ways is precisely what one seeks to do in the prioritization of academic programs.

Bob Dickeson is uniquely equipped to offer a road map for setting and shaping academic priorities. He has been there: as a faculty member, as an academic administrator, as president, and as one who has been at the interface of higher education and state government. He understands and articulates the crucial role played by boards of trustees. He has seen us from the perspective of the private sector, including that of the USA Group, where he now resides. Through it all, Dickeson has gained an appreciation for the vast diversity of American higher education and the almost impossible job of shaping and setting academic priorities. Nonetheless, in this book, he makes the complex simple, the abstract concrete.

All members of the academic community should read this book: presidents and provosts most of all, but trustees and faculty members, deans and department chairs, prospective donors, and higher education policymakers as well. There is a valuable message for all audiences: as difficult as it is, the campuses of this country must do a better job of setting academic priorities and managing costs.

The forces that frustrate the prioritization of academic needs are legion. Vested interests on campus and pressure groups off campus emerge from nowhere. Try to close an academic program, no matter how humble, and suddenly you will find it is among the top ten in the nation and at the very center of the institution's mission. Beyond the vested interests, however, institutional governance mechanisms work too slowly, and sometimes not at all, as the desire to expand or change the academic program confronts the desire to preserve and sustain it.

Making judgments about academic quality and the centrality of academic programs to the campus character and mission is, by its very nature, an ambiguous assignment. Such judgments are always open to challenge. Bob Dickeson, however, makes a compelling case for setting academic priorities; issues a call for leadership to trustees, presidents, and faculty members; and suggests an orderly process supported by a sound conceptual framework. In short, he helps make the impossible achievable.

Prioritizing academic programs will not happen, he counsels, in the absence of informed and courageous leadership from the president, the provost, the faculty, and the trustees. It is to the empowerment of those academic leaders that this book speaks. Although simply doing a better job of shaping and setting academic program priorities will not alone assure the quality and access in

higher education that is essential to 21st century America, failure
to set priorities more effectively will almost certainly place academic quality and access at risk.

February 1999   Stanley O. Ikenberry
                                         President
                                         American Council on Education

To the four extraordinary women in my life:
Ludie, Betsy, Cindy, and Whitley

Preface

The initial idea for this book emerged from my experience as a rookie university president trying to cut costs in a turbulent time. The institution I inherited had already taken the "fortuitous cuts" that were available, chopped administrative units, and tried the politically expedient but academically unsound approach of across-the-board cuts for several years. As I pieced together a plan to re-allocate resources among the academic programs of the university, from the weakest to the strongest, I was struck by the dearth of helpful literature in the field about how to prioritize in a responsible way. I vowed that if I survived the process, I would make available to other institutions the lessons I had learned.

Over the next decade, about fifty other colleges and universities solicited copies of our process and the plan that resulted from it because they too confronted the reality that they could not be all things to all people. In the drive to downsize (or, as one colleague euphemistically called it, "rightsize") an institution, there is precious little in the way of effective guidance. Most institutions confronting the issue of reallocating program resources are meandering into an academic minefield, often without a detector.

As president of a consulting firm for the next six years, my colleagues and I worked with hundreds of colleges and universities, all trying to accomplish the impossible: to achieve higher levels of excellence in more and more academic programs with scarcer resources. What these institutions needed was a tighter focus. The application of my system, tailored to and enhanced by many of these institutions, has been strengthened to the point where I now want to share it with all higher education leaders—faculty, administrators, board members, public policy shapers—who care about the appropriate balance between quality and quantity in American higher education.

The need for tighter focus is critical in higher education. So is the need to restore public trust about costs. Indeed the public policy debate is shifting markedly from questions about access to those of affordability. It has been my experience that higher education leaders are quite willing to respond to national calls for controlling costs and to make change happen to increase their credibility when convinced it is in the best interest of their institutions to do so. *But they lack the proper tools*. It is one thing to call for reform; it is another to guide the way toward achieving it. This book is designed to serve as that guide.

The ideas here are not mine alone. My initial plan has been reshaped by thousands of faculty members, department chairs, deans, vice presidents, presidents, and board members at private and public colleges and universities across the country who have applied these principles to their unique situations. The ideas have been honed by my campus, consulting, corporate, government, and foundation colleagues over the years and refined by practice and implementation in multiple settings. These suggestions are stronger for having been tempered by experience, exposure to criticism, the fires of campus debate and action, and the courage of leaders willing to act on them to improve their institutions.

Throughout the book I make numerous references to the experiences and actions of the colleges and universities that undertook this kind of academic reform. Their telling adds a believable, personal dimension to otherwise cold recommendations. The relationship between an institution and a consultant must revere confidentiality, however, and thus the examples I cite, which represent real-life people, places, and situations, are disguised so as to honor that relationship. I hope readers will bear with my descriptors, such as "small private college" and "land grant university," and in any quest to figure out *who* will not miss the intended lesson about *why*.

Overview of the Contents

One can infer from the contents of this book an agenda for colleges and universities. In its essence, the first chapter seeks to make the case for real academic reform. Portions of it may prove useful in building awareness for campus constituencies that are somehow sheltered from the external clamor for reform or the internal reality of underfunded visions. At a time when even the richest, best-endowed universities in the land are admitting to insufficient resources to retain their program offerings with quality, it is no wonder that the other thirty-five hundred institutions must confess to proportionate inadequacies. Many institutions can probably survive by maintaining the status quo, but only by reallocating resources will they flourish. And reallocation, to be done well, requires appropriate prioritization.

The finest, most sophisticated system for analyzing academic programs will absolutely fail unless it is championed by strong leaders armed with a clarified mission. Thus Chapters Two and Three focus on what steps the campus must undertake to reaffirm its mission and what leadership it can count on (including from its board) to complete prioritization successfully.

The balance of the book provides a step-by-step guide for confronting the many dimensions of academic program prioritization. Programs, after all, constitute the intellectual and service drivers of institutional life, and they consume valuable resources. Chapters Four through Eight set out specific, campus-based suggestions and lessons learned from the academic trenches. These chapters also answer a lot of practical questions. What constitutes an academic program? What are the most valid criteria to use in measuring programs? How should measurement and analysis be undertaken? What issues and questions can be anticipated throughout the process? Once decisions are made, how are they to be implemented?

The final chapter presents the entire process within a systematic context. Academic prioritization (or any other academic process, for that matter) operates at the confluence of multiple forces. Understanding the nature and relative impact of these forces will permit the many stakeholders in American higher education to make more informed judgments about how a specific institution is reconciling its competing internal and external demands.

Specific campus-based case studies are excerpted in the resources at the end of the book. They are not intended as models of ideal solutions (each institution must arrive at its own conclusion about its future), but they are meant to reveal the specifics of how some colleges and universities are coping with the realities of resource reallocation at the same time they are reclaiming public credibility about their accountability.

Audience

This book is written for all those who practice and who care about higher education. Reallocation of resources requires careful priority setting. "What to keep?" "What to abandon?" What to reduce?" What to strengthen?" are perplexing questions that should confront all academic leaders. Presidents, chief academic officers, and deans will want to use the materials provided here to help build awareness, craft their own change methodology, make the tough but necessary decisions, and thereby improve their institutions. Leaders of nonacademic programs in student services, academic support, administrative operations, and institutional advancement can readily adapt these processes and criteria to their reallocation imperatives as well.

"Academic leadership" also includes faculty, particularly faculty members serving in administrative or campus governance roles. The wisest department chairs, for example, can prepare for a pending reallocation by anticipating the 150 questions relevant to the program prioritization criteria and assembling plans and documentation that cast their department's programs in the best possible light. (There is nothing like going into a test knowing the questions in advance.) Even if a program reallocation is not likely, forthrightly addressing the criteria outlined in Chapter Five will help reveal an academic blueprint for departmental accreditation, self-study, or continuous quality improvement purposes.

Members of institutional governing boards, who alone exercise the final authority for program additions and deletions, should use this book as a continuing reference to gauge the breadth and depth of the thinking behind the recommendations brought to them. Although board members will not want to micromanage, they require the knowledge this book offers them to ask hard questions about program costs, quality, coherence, and centrality. The judicious use of the book's lessons should permit a college or university to save time and money, reduce agony, and enhance quality.

Finally, public policymakers are an intended audience. At federal and state levels, policy and allocation leaders want colleges to contain spiraling costs, improve student learning (particularly for undergraduates), foster stronger college-community connections, and adapt to the changing demands of the new information technology. This book offers productive alternatives to mindless cutting or faculty bashing. The real culprit is the needless proliferation of programs. Policymakers can become better equipped to understand the complex dynamics of administering universities and push for rationality and accountability at the same time that they honor institutional values and autonomy.

I sincerely hope the book enables all readers to understand the scope of the reallocation problem, believe in the effectiveness of the prioritization solution, and summon the requisite courage to strengthen their institutions.

Acknowledgments

Although I am solely responsible for this book, its evolution has been directly and indirectly fostered by many others. I am indebted to USA Group, Inc., of Indiana, its board of directors, and its president and CEO, James C. Lintzenich, for their steadfast and generous support of the USA Group Foundation. This work is made possible because of the foundation's sponsorship. Martha D.

Lamkin, executive vice president for corporate advancement of USA Group, and co-instigator of the foundation, was an invaluable partner in this work. Martha insisted I write the book, encouraged me each step of the way, and used her considerable writing talent to provide valuable editing in the final stages.

The original program prioritization I undertook in 1981–1982 would not have succeeded without the creative talents and academic judgments of Charles W. Manning, Robert L. Heiny, Joan Richardson, John L. Burke, David J. Figuli, and Robert B. Stein. Nor would the results have been implemented without the courageous and dependable commitment to quality by board members Thomas C. Stokes, Gail Schoettler, Betsy B. Karowsky, Beverly L. Biffle, Richard G. Trahan, and Shari Williams and state officials Richard D. Lamm and Lee R. Kerschner. Subsequent iterations and improvements in the prioritization process were measurably assisted by the faculty, staff, and board members at the scores of institutions that undertook reallocation. These academic pioneers must remain anonymous, of course, but I am deeply indebted to them.

Through the years, my administrative understanding has been shaped and challenged by strong mentors and professional colleagues in numerous education, government, business, and consultative settings. I particularly acknowledge Elmer Ellis, Thomas A. Brady, Robert Callis, A. T. "Jack" Matthews, J. Lawrence Walkup, Virgil W. Gillenwater, Governor Bruce Babbitt, Lee R. Kerschner, Robert C. Albrecht, James E. Walker, Jessica S. Kozloff, W. Clark Hendley, Nancy A. Scott, Governor Richard D. Lamm, Governor Roy Romer, Gary H. Quehl, Lee R. Noel, Randi S. Levitz, Stanley J. Spanbauer, and Thomas E. Williams. I have also been influenced by the teaching and examples set by Lloyd M. Wells, Richard S. Kirkendall, Glen T. Nygreen, Ernest L. Boyer, Frank Newman, and Harold Enarson.

I was fortunate to have secured the insights and penetrating criticism of outstanding readers who took time from their active schedules to raise questions, point out flaws, and suggest parts of the manuscript that needed elaboration: Russell Edgerton, Jessica S.

Kozloff, Robert L. Heiny, James E. Walker, Lee R. Noel, Gary H. Quehl, John L. Nies, Tracy L. Wolff, and Martha D. Lamkin. This book is stronger for their shared wisdom.

Thanks go to Jean Rose for her editorial expertise; Lisa Cole, Mary Wright, and Natasha Swingley for their technical assistance; Sara Murray-Plumer and Susan O. Conner for their valuable advice; and the qualified staff of the Indiana University–Purdue University Indianapolis Library for their help.

I am grateful to Gale Erlandson, senior editor for the Higher and Adult Education Series, and David Brightman, editorial assistant at Jossey-Bass Publishers, for their encouragement and capable assistance. Jossey-Bass also provided additional, anonymous readers whose insightful ideas proved valuable.

I am indebted to Stan Ikenberry for his thought-provoking and generous foreword.

Ludmila Weir Dickeson deserves special recognition for making important suggestions to clarify key points in the manuscript, for supporting this effort with warmth, love, and encouragement, and for putting up with me for thirty-five years.

Indianapolis   Robert C. Dickeson
February 1999

The Author

Robert C. Dickeson is senior vice president for corporate advancement of USA Group, Inc., and heads the USA Group Foundation, a philanthropic organization that is dedicated to improving higher education.

His career has included service in higher education, government, and business. Dickeson has taught at the University of Missouri, Northern Arizona University, Arizona State University, the University of Northern Colorado, and the University of Colorado–Denver. He served as dean, vice provost, and vice president at Northern Arizona University (1969–1979) and as president of the University of Northern Colorado (1981–1991). He served as director of the Department of Administration and chair of the governor's cabinet in Arizona (1979–1981) and chief of staff, chair of the governor's cabinet and executive director of the Colorado Office of State Planning and Budget (1987).

From 1991 to 1997 he was president and CEO of Noel-Levitz Centers, Inc. (now USA Group Noel Levitz), the higher education consulting and services firm. From 1995 to 1997 he was division president of Management Services for USA Enterprises, Inc.

Dickeson has chaired blue-ribbon commissions appointed by three governors in two states; has been an officer of thirty corporate, government, foundation, or public affairs organizations; and has served in various roles with the American Council on Education, the American Association of State Colleges and Universities, and the Education Commission of the States. He was a charter member of the President's Forum on Teaching as a Profession and a cofounder of the Renaissance Group of Universities. His numerous awards include recognition from the American Association of Colleges of Teacher Education, the American Association of State Colleges and Universities, and the North Central Intercollegiate Athletic Conference.

The author of numerous publications in the fields of higher education leadership and policy and public administration, Dickeson has extensive consulting experiences with private and public two- and four-year colleges and universities and for-profit and non-profit organizations throughout the United States. He is a member of the editorial advisory board of *Net Results: The NASPA Leadership and Strategy Magazine*, an on-line journal of the National Association of Student Personnel Administrators, and is executive editor of the *USA Group Foundation New Agenda Series*.

Chapter One

Recognizing the Need for Reform

> The most likely source for needed resources is
> reallocation of existing resources.

American higher education is regarded universally as the best in the world. Yet American higher education *institutions* are overwhelmed by competing demands, internal and external, that threaten the capacity of higher education to meet ever increasing expectations. The contrast between internal and external pressures could not be more illustrative of the need for reform.

Internal Pressures

Internally colleges and universities are under increasing pressure to accomplish four things: increase revenues, decrease expenses, improve quality, and strengthen reputation. They have been particularly successful at raising revenues. Revenues required to fuel the collegiate enterprise have risen dramatically as campuses have tried to cover increases in enrollments, inflation, faculty salaries, additional programs and services, shrinking state budget support (in the case of public institutions), and institutional student financial aid to improve access (in the case of private institutions).

Increasing Revenues

Jerry S. Davis, in his book, *College Affordability: A Closer Look at the Crisis* (1997), summarizes the growth of tuition as the major factor in overall revenue increases over the decade ending in 1993:

It is apparent that even if tuition had continued to defray a constant percentage of [current fund expenditures], inflation in those expenditures would have resulted in substantial growth in tuition charges. About 56 percent of the total growth in tuition revenue between 1984 and 1993 can be attributed to inflation and enrollment growth, 19 percent can be attributed to spending beyond amounts needed to match inflation, and the remaining 25 percent is attributable to tuitions defraying a greater share of college expenditures [p. 22].

Later studies continue to confirm that although tuition increases may be increasing at a decreasing rate (that was the trend from 1993 to 1996), the overall price for admission is still outpacing most indicators of inflation and the pocketbooks of most American families. Stated as a ratio, the average undergraduate price for tuition, fees, and room and board compared to median family income jumped from 0.14 in 1977 to 0.21 in 1996 (Stringer, Cunningham, O'Brien, and Merisotis, 1998).

Revenue is also increasing through substantial and successful efforts to tap the generosity of donors. Donations to educational institutions, including colleges and universities, increased by 12.3 percent for the last report year (1997) at the same time that overall charitable giving in the United States increased by 7.49 percent (*Giving USA*, 1998). Many institutions are undertaking capital campaigns with goals in the multiples of millions of dollars. The development office is one of the fastest-growing departments at many institutions as the thirst for revenue continues unslaked.

Decreasing Expenses

The institutional quest to cut expenses has been less dramatic. Institutions typically attempt to make budget ends meet on the expense side by not filling positions, curtailing or deferring certain expenditures, and implementing across-the-board cuts in operating budgets for departments. These efforts are traditionally short term in nature and are designed to "get through another budget year." By contrast, several current practices have made some inroads into needed collegiate cost containment. Benchmarking—the practice of comparing best practices in management with one's own—has been the subject of creative effort by the National Association of College and University Business Officers (NACUBO). Working with Coopers & Lybrand, NACUBO has developed since 1991 a process of sharing information among several hundred participating institutions. A database of institutional practice permits measurement and comparison of work processes in several internal functions, activities, or operations. Such administrative activities as processing an application for admission or processing a purchase order have received sophisticated analysis for "business process reengineering" (NACUBO, 1994; Douglas, Shaw, and Shepko, 1997).

Another promising area for cost containment is privatizing, or outsourcing non-mission-critical functions of the institution, presumably at a savings. The growth of outsourcing in higher education, although it does not parallel the practice in other organizations (notably business and government), is significant. My own review of this subject revealed some twenty-three different functions that colleges and universities have outsourced to noncollegiate providers. A list of these functions, together with critical questions that institutions should answer before proceeding with outsourcing, is contained in Resource A.

Still another promising practice is the growing movement toward activity-based costing (ABC) in higher education. A cost accounting system that seeks to determine accurately the full costs of services and products, ABC has recently been applied to college settings. By identifying "activity centers," or revenue and cost units, and assigning resource costs, institutions can identify outputs or cost objects, thus more strictly connecting costs with results. This tool can be especially effective in budgeting, evaluation, reporting, and pricing decisions (Lundquist, 1996; Trussel and Bitner, 1996).

An interesting insight into the financial viability of higher education is available by reviewing the changes in college bond and other debt ratings, made periodically by the public finance departments of investors service bureaus. One recent report, by Moody's, notes that although there is a generally stable outlook for higher education, certain trends are noteworthy, among them the following:

- For more than a decade, tuition increases have far exceeded corresponding increases in family income. The potential for future tuition increases is limited, which will reduce operating flexibility.
- Private institutions face the challenge of spiraling financial aid costs and an increasing tendency to "buy" students through generous financial aid awards.
- Schools are increasingly recognizing the need to control both administrative and academic costs. Only a handful, however, have actually implemented academic cost-cutting measures [Moody's, 1996, p. 1].

Benchmarking, outsourcing, and newer cost accounting techniques have proven successful for some institutions. In most cases, however, real cost-containment efforts have thus far avoided significant penetration into the sacred precincts of the academic side of the higher education enterprise.

Increasing Quality and Strengthening Reputation

Higher education's other two internal objectives—increasing quality and strengthening reputation—are perceived by campus faculty and staff not only to be at severe odds with the cost-cutting objective, but absolutely essential to the imperative to increase revenues. And it is here that the dilemma tightens. Quality in higher education has usually been measured by inputs: degrees held by the faculty, number of volumes in the library, and, today's measure, the degree of campus-wide access to the Internet. These are all costly items. Traditional definitions of reputation are harder to measure, but it is clear that colleges and universities have been adding programs, services, equipment, buildings, and public relations efforts to achieve greater reputational prominence. By so doing, they hope to attract more (and better) students, a higher-quality profile among its faculty, and the heightened interest of generous donors.

How to reconcile these competing objectives internally, in addition to the fundamental and simultaneous battle over allocation of scarce resources among the competing *purposes* of higher education—teaching, research, and service—is anomalous indeed. And then there are the external pressures.

External Pressures

Externally, American higher education is experiencing a firestorm of public criticism. Demands for increased accountability have been consistently advanced in a number of public forums throughout the United States.

Federal Demands

In 1992, the U.S. Congress made over one hundred changes in the Higher Education Act to address fraud and abuse by postsecondary institutions receiving the benefits from Title IV federal financial programs. Among the changes Congress planned during the 1992 reauthorization was the empowerment of fifty state postsecondary review entities (SPREs), earlier authorized in the Higher Education Act of 1965, with the purpose of implementing the federal statutory standards. Although this implementation has been temporarily shelved (due to lack of funding and strong opposition from the higher education community), the standards that underpin the SPREs have not. A review of the fifteen standards reveals the inherent distrust that the Congress, at least, has for postsecondary institutions: the adequacy of information provided to prospective students; the appropriateness of student assessment; the relationship of tuition and fees to employment-related programs; the appropriateness of credit or clock hours required to complete programs; the fairness and equity of refund policies to protect students. The list goes on. Although it is true that the targets of most of these demands are some proprietary schools (for-profit career schools), the postsecondary community at large is harnessed with these mandates and painted with the same brush of distrust. It is clear, even from the response of the established higher education community to SPREs, that the real issue was not only accountability but institutional integrity (American Association of Community Colleges and others, 1993).

In every successive session of Congress, there have been new calls for increasing higher education accountability. Legislation has been advanced to limit tuition increases, impose tuition caps, or peg tuition to the Consumer Price Index. There have been new demands for cost containment and for tightening audit requirements, and new challenges have been issued to higher education's vaunted tax-exempt status. The 1998 reauthorization of the Higher Education Act will require increased institutional reporting to the public on prices and costs (a mandate that will only add to administrative costs).

State Demands

The federal government has not been alone in impressing these demands. A survey conducted by the Public Higher Education Program at the Rockefeller Institute of Government in 1997 found heightened state government interest in these issues as well (Burke and Serban, 1997). Ten states currently have performance funding (defined for survey purposes as "special state funding tied directly to the achievements of public colleges and universities on specific performance indicators"), and eighteen more states are likely to adopt such a program in the next five years (Burke and Serban, 1997, pp. 1–3). Both performance funding and performance budgeting focus attention (and public-funded support) on key indicators of institutional performance. Although the indicators vary by state, they include such items as enrollment and graduation rates, time to degree, retention rates, effectiveness of remediation activities, transfer rates, job placement data, minority graduation rates, and faculty workload and productivity.

These government-sanctioned approaches to the funding and oversight of higher education would have been unthinkable a generation ago because they would have been perceived as unnecessary. Today, by contrast, such approaches are regarded as too little by most legislators and too intrusive by most college administrators.

National Calls for Accountability

The calls for greater accountability have not been limited to governmental entities. A variety of blue ribbon commissions and research institute reports have focused attention on the issue of rising costs and the concomitant demand for institutional accountability. The Commission on National Investment in Higher Education, for example, composed not of opponents to higher education but rather some of its most eminent leaders and supporters, reported in 1997 that the current situation represented a "time bomb ticking under the nation's social and economic foundations." "At a time," the commission reported, "when the level of education needed for productive employment is increasing, the opportunity to go to college will be denied to millions of Americans unless sweeping changes are made to control costs, halt sharp increases in tuition, and increase other sources of revenue." Among its recommendations, the commission stressed the need for institutions of higher education to "make major structural changes in their governance system so that decision makers can assess the relative value of departments, programs, and systems in order to reallocate scarce resources." Other recommendations included calling for political leaders to reallocate resources toward education, institutions to pursue greater mission differentiation, colleges and universities to develop sharing arrangements to improve productivity, and a redefinition of the appropriate level of education for all citizens to include some form of postsecondary education or training (*Breaking the Social Contract*, 1997).

For some the solution is to attack governance systems; for others it is to attack the very faculty who deliver the world's best system of higher education. "Faculty bashing" through attacks on tenure or on faculty resistance to downsizing has been given credence in the popular press (Honan, 1998).

The Commission on Costs

The clamor for colleges to act more responsibly reached a climax in 1998 with the publication of the report of the National Commission on the Cost of Higher Education. Formed by the Congress as an independent advisory body under Public Law 105–18 (Title IV, Cost of Higher Education Review, 1997), the commission's activities and recommendations represented the highest level of public policy concern about college costs to date. The commission noted that instructional cost per student had increased from 1987 to 1996 by an average of 57 percent for public four-year colleges and universities, 69 percent for private four-year institutions, and 52 percent for public two-year colleges. At the same time, tuition increased for all three institutional categories at a rate faster than instructional cost per student (132 percent, 99 percent, and 85 percent, respectively). Although some of the disparity between increases in price and increases in cost may be explained by downward shifts in the subsidies that institutions receive (internal or external subsidies), the impression left with the public is that institutions are increasingly greedy.

To deal with this and other of its concerns, the commission presented a five-part action agenda with forty-two recommendations in five areas:

1. Strengthen institutional cost control.

2. Improve market information and public accountability.

3. Deregulate higher education.

4. Rethink accreditation.

5. Enhance and simplify federal student aid.

No fewer than ten specific recommendations—more than for any other part of the national commission's action agenda—related to cutting or controlling costs in higher education. At the same time, the commission included in its final report an "unfinished agenda," which addressed the need for a more thorough analysis of academic programs, levels of instruction, faculty load distribution, and other issues that are the focus of this book (National Commission on the Cost of Higher Education, 1998).

The commission's findings were informed, in part, by the early results of the American Council on Education's (ACE) public opinion survey about price and affordability in higher education. Survey results were shared with the commission at its November 1997 meeting in Nashville. The full survey results, ultimately published by ACE in 1998, reinforced the extraordinary gap that exists between public interest in and understanding about college price, costs, and affordability. At a time when 57 percent of the public thinks colleges are not charging a fair price for a college education and 80 percent actually believe most colleges and universities make a profit, it is indeed time for higher education to focus serious attention on correcting the misinformation and fixing the costs problem (American Council on Education, 1998; Ikenberry and Hartle, 1998).

The Case for Reform

Thus, from forces both internal and external to higher education comes the clear and compelling message: *there is a fundamental need to reform.* The status quo is unacceptable. The efforts of the past, however well intentioned, have been insufficient because they have focused for the most part solely on the nonacademic portion of the higher education enterprise.

This book is based on seven postulates:

1. Academic programs (such as degrees offered) are not only the heart of the collegiate institution; they constitute the real drivers of cost for the entire enterprise, academic and nonacademic.

2. Academic programs have been permitted to grow, and in some cases calcify, on the institutional body without critical regard to their relative worth.

3. Most institutions are unrealistically striving to be all things to all people in their quest for students, reputation, and support rather than focusing their resources on the mission and programs that they can accomplish with distinction.

4. There is growing incongruence between the academic programs offered and the resources required to mount them with quality, and most institutions are thus overprogrammed for their available resources.

5. Traditional approaches, like across-the-board cuts, tend to mediocrity for all programs.

6. The most likely source for needed resources is reallocation of existing resources, from weakest to strongest programs.

7. Reallocation cannot be appropriately accomplished without rigorous, effective, and academically responsible prioritization.

If these postulates are well-founded, then prioritization is a necessary process to accomplish reform. Fundamental to an understanding of the need for prioritization, however, is an equally clear understanding of the barriers to prioritization.

Academic programs—and the capital and services required to mount them—constitute the overwhelming majority of current funds expenditures at any college or university. In addition to instructional costs (at 30.5 percent the most sizable single expenditure for all types of institutions), other expenditure categories, such as academic support (6.7 percent), research (9.4 percent), and public service (3.7 percent), also flow directly from the academic programs offered by a collegiate institution (U.S. Department of Education, 1997). Other institutional expenses (institutional support and plant and maintenance, for example) are indirectly affected by academic offerings. Yet a careful examination of this highly important area of the budget has been obscured or, at worst, prevented, for several reasons.

Overblown Marketing

First, institutions' own marketing efforts to induce students to enroll have driven the accretion of academic offerings for several years. Colleges, in a quest to beat the competition, claim in their viewbooks and catalogues that the institution offers a "program"—whether a full-blown degree, a minor, an emphasis area, or even a course or two—in some new specialty designed to attract students. This pattern of outbidding the competition academically is both costly, because new faculty, library holdings and equipment, or support services may accompany the addition, and usually futile. As Alexander Astin at UCLA has pointed out for over twenty years now, incoming freshmen are much more concerned about other institutional characteristics—"very good academic reputation," "graduates get good jobs," "size of college," "offered financial assistance," to name the top four—than they are about the specific academic specialty available (Astin, 1998). As everyone who has counseled incoming freshmen knows, most newcomers are undecided about a college major, and of those who think they know, most change their minds—and majors—within the first two years.

Yet the pressure to add choices to the academic menu continues on the misassumption that students will be magnetically attracted to the campus by new program offerings and will somehow disregard the other, more salient reasons for choosing a college. The plain truth is that for the most part, adding academic programs results in a substantial *diminution of resources for existing programs* and has very little to do with attracting students, particularly at the freshman level.

Institutions add programs in part because of a genuine desire to be of service. Higher education has become a market-driven enterprise, where the consumer is sovereign. Growth of academic programs is understandable. Higher education is in high demand. And demand can be expressed in ways that cause institutions, eager to survive and to flourish, to respond. What often results is a lack of focus.

Nonacademic programs proliferate as well. Today's students bring to the campus expectations for services and amenities that more nearly resemble resort-like, not monastic, lifestyles. The institutional criticism—of trying to be all things to all people—resonates on many campuses nationally.

Runaway Specialization

Academic programs also burgeon because of the specialized interests of the faculty. Individuals who come to the professorate bring distinctive interests and academic preferences with them. One may be hired to teach Freshman English, but it is Austronesian and Papuan languages that ignite the scholarly imagination. Within every academic department debates rage about adding new courses that will fulfill the needs of individual faculty members who want to teach them. In large part, this is how curriculum develops. New concepts, new ancillary but related fields, and new interdisciplinary twists all arise and confront traditional approaches. The fund of knowledge is growing exponentially, and with it come new subjects for legitimate inquiry and new challenges to the existing phyla of a discipline's offerings. Academic disciplines do not sit still. Perhaps new faculty members have been promised, as a part of the hiring process, new courses to fit their specialties.

Once colleges shifted historically from a curriculum composed solely of required courses in favor of adding more and more electives, the accretion exploded. Department meetings on curriculum often represent power struggles among members; voting blocs form around various and sundry causes—occasionally academic—and courses may be ushered into the curriculum for internal political reasons. Mutual back-scratching feels good to all legislative bodies. New courses are often sold internally to campuswide curriculum committees, which hold sway on these matters, as pilot or experimental courses. Nobody can be against giving the new course on Esoterica 101 a chance. "If you build it, will the students come?" The notion is to try it to see what happens. The trouble is that many college catalogues resemble stables containing hobbyhorses of battles past. This curriculum creep is, unfortunately, only incremental, not decremental. There are precious few internal processes to handle the elimination of courses that no longer make sense or meet student needs.

Unhealthy Internal Competition

Curriculum creep thus leads to *program creep*. In an era of tight resources, scarcity results in intense competition. Academic departments vie for resources—faculty lines; classroom, laboratory, and office space; equipment; and travel dollars—and compete with colleague departments as both functional and allocational rivals. When resources are limited, collaborative efforts across departments suffer. Interdisciplinary initiatives suffer. Collegiality suffers. Departments become fiefdoms, unwilling to cede credits, programs, or the precious coin of the realm, the student FTE (full-time equivalent). (If one full-time student takes fifteen credits per term, that is somehow "equivalent" to five students taking three credits per term. This concept, a triumph of mathematics over common sense, is misused and abused on almost all college campuses. It is an example of our desire to measure things that are easy to measure rather than things that are appropriate to measure.) Balkanization of the academy results.

Program creep is not unakin to *mission creep*. As institutions take on more and more programs, attempting to meet more and more demands, aspirations sometimes overtake reality. With just a few more programs, two-year colleges could become four-year colleges. With just a few more graduate programs, teaching institutions could become regional or possibly research institutions. This quest for more status and prestige is seen as helping improve an institution's relative position on the academic food chain. A recently published job description for a public university presidency included the declared institutional aspiration to move from a Carnegie classification as Research II to Research I. In any given year, a collegiate athletic program at the NCAA Division II level will toy with the aspirational (and costly) notion of moving to Division I, even though the school cannot afford it. The same phenomenon prevails in academic affairs. Faculty in a department offering a baccalaureate in a particular field lust after the offering of a more prestigious—and expensive—master's degree.

Growth is the operational paradigm for higher education. Institutional presidents are greeted by—and indeed greet each other with—the questions: "How's your enrollment? Did it grow?" Growth of enrollment means growth in revenues. Growth in revenues often leads to growth in programs. Program proliferation feeds the institution's appetite for growth in aspiration. And institutions, overly programmed for their resources, raise prices to satiate the appetites.

Following the Money

Overprogramming may also result from the beneficence of others. Institutions, public as well as private, have become increasingly sophisticated in their fundraising abilities to generate major gifts and capital support, but the results sometimes come at a price. Campuses prefer unrestricted gifts, which permit paying bills where the need is greatest. Donors, on the other hand, prefer to restrict gifts: to named scholarships, to favored programs, to sponsored research, or, in the case of extremely large gifts, to fund an entirely new program (such as a center or an institute), which becomes a continuing, and often costly, obligation of the college. The albatross may be on the endangered species list, but several can be found on some campuses.

The phenomenon of directing the mission toward available resources is synonymous with the history of American higher education. Like parched travelers on an academic desert, campus officials will change course in the direction of the divining rod toward any life-sustaining water. A typical issue of the *Chronicle of Higher Education* will report a dozen or more new academic programs being established weekly, inaugurated by gifts of well-meaning donors, foundations, and corporations. The more successful the campus is at generating such tightly restricted gifts, the more likely that its programs, expectations, and mission will proliferate.

Disconnected Planning

Still another reason for the lack of attention to academic programs is the reality that most campus strategic plans are flawed. Having reviewed scores of such plans, it is clear to me that less than 20 percent of them mention where the required resources are going to come from; fewer still identify "reallocation of existing resources" as a likely source to tap. Strategic plans have become purely additive: after months or years of analysis, campuses come up with unrealistic wish lists, encompassing new programs, new equipment, new buildings, new services, new faculty, new staff, and new initiatives. These plans tend to assume several things: (1) the status quo as a given, with all current programs composing the baseline, (2) all programs, goals, and objectives are to be "maintained" or "enhanced," but rarely diminished or eliminated, (3) if resources are mentioned at all, they are to be enhanced by hiking tuition, increasing enrollment, securing more appropriations or grants, or raising more money, or all of these, and (4) all planning goals are equal in weight and importance and thus lack priority. This is neither planning nor strategic.

Faculty Resistance

Finally, a serious review of academic programming is often prevented because of anticipated resistance from the faculty. Academic programs have taken on a sacrosanct aura, and the reasons for this impediment are complex and intertwined.

It is a long-standing tradition of higher education that academic programs enjoy relative independence and autonomy. It is axiomatic that a faculty, duly credentialed, is vested with the wide authority to determine what and how academic subjects are to be taught. Curricular power is not easily or readily relinquished. The culture of the academy values noninterference. The prioritization of academic programs, for example, of declaring that some programs are superior to others, is anathema to the academy.

The whole notion of prioritizing also violates the egalitarian ideology in higher education. The mantra for such ideology goes something like this: "If all programs are more or less equal, who's to judge their relative worth? I'm an expert in one discipline, and I rely on my colleague experts in other disciplines to do their work. I am just as incapable of judging the value of their work or the worth of their programs as they obviously are of judging mine. Our common mistrust of administrators to do anything right unites us in opposition to management efforts to poke around in, and likely destroy, what we've worked so hard to establish."

The principal line-item expense in academic programs is personnel costs. People. Jobs. Careers. It is small wonder that a faculty would be reluctant to take on a review that might conclude in a reduction of programs, populated by faculty. College and university faculty are usually not interchangeable, contrary to the case in elementary or even secondary education. A cut in sections of the fourth grade will find teachers willing and able to teach fifth grade. By contrast, the very academic specialization that college faculty members cherish works to their detriment when programs are cut. Institutional flexibility is limited. Although it is possible to retrain faculty in some disciplines for the purpose of internal relocation to positions where demand might be greater, the occurrence of such shifts is rare. The problem is exacerbated by overly generous tenure practices. A large number of academic departments in the nation are "tenured up," where past tenure practice has filled every available personnel slot with a tenured faculty member, thus limiting flexibility in reducing positions. Additional pressures come from legal challenges to mandatory retirement policies. Faced with reducing costs in a labor-intensive enterprise like higher education and confronted by the extraordinary reluctance to remove tenured faculty, many institutions feel hamstrung in their efforts to get control.

Nor are egalitarianism or job security imperatives the sole barriers to change. Most faculty feel an intense sense of stewardship for their programs. Some programs have been around for decades. Faculty rightly feel they are responsible for the continuity and stability of a program that they inherited from academic predecessors, on whose intellectual shoulders current faculty stand. Graduates of the program, as well as its current students, have vested interests in seeing that programs thrive. Many programs have other relationships—with community or national groups, for example—that are difficult, if not impossible, to slough off.

Reconciling Competing Demands

And yet despite the obstacles, change must occur. Colleges and universities have evolved to the point where the bloated curriculum is receiving inadequate resources to accomplish its purposes. I have yet to hear a department head or dean among the several hundred I have met over the years who feels her or his programs are adequately funded. Most academic programs are seriously undernourished. Keeping up with qualified faculty and adequate support staff is difficult. It is nearly impossible to provide equipment necessary to mount the program in a respectable way, particularly in an age of rapid technological transformation. Conducting programs in facilities that are in their worst shape in American history is ludicrous. *The price for academic program bloat for all is impoverishment of each.*

It is time to recognize that colleges and universities must get a better handle on expenses. To date, most of the effort has been to (1) focus on the administrative, nonacademic portions of the institution, (2) defer maintenance of the physical plant to the point that recovery becomes financially unfeasible, (3) ignore the academic program side as too politically volatile to touch, and (4) make necessary budget cuts across the board so that all programs suffer equally (egalitarianism, again), which is politically expedient on campus but academically repugnant.

Leslie and Fretwell (1996) in their thirteen-campus review of diverse colleges and universities undergoing hard times found that although budget cuts had been made and furloughs implemented, no real program cuts had been made.

The inescapable truth is that not all programs are equal. Some are more efficient. Some are more effective. Some are more central to the mission of the institution. And yet insufficient effort has gone into forthrightly addressing and acting on the efficiency, effectiveness, and essentiality of academic programs.

The imperative for American higher education is to undertake a program-by-program review of all academic offerings, and to do so simultaneously, since all such offerings feed at the resources trough simultaneously. Programs should be measured with an eye toward their relative value, so that reallocation can be facilitated. Because the most likely source of resources is the reallocation of existing resources, and because much of the institution's very being is at stake, the process for accomplishing prioritization must be academically responsible and honorable. This is no time for campus politics as usual.

What will also be required is an institutional culture concerned enough about its future that it exhibits the will to act. Understanding the culture, acting on the challenge to improve the institution, and empowering all stakeholders to participate fully in such a transformation will require leadership. Without effective leadership, there is no likelihood that the institution's best efforts will be motivated or inspired.

Chapter Two

Identifying Responsible Leadership

> When the best leaders' work is done the people say,
> "We did it ourselves."
>
> —*Lao-tzu*

Leadership, like computer technology, is moving toward a more distributed model in modern organizations. Even colleges and universities are recognizing the growing emergence and interdependence of leaders at all levels throughout the organization. The shift from a strictly hierarchical to a distributed system of leadership has both promises and challenges as higher education institutions confront critical issues. From the point of view of prioritizing academic programs, an early assessment of the extent and quality of institutional leadership is essential to uncover three things: the sources of impetus for needed change, the strength of resolve in seeing change through to fruition, and the need to affix the appropriate balance between responsibility and authority.

Sources of Reform

In my experience, the impetus for reform in the area of institution-wide academic program reallocation comes from one of three sources: the president, the governing board, or the provost.

The President

Ideally the college or university president operates at the confluence of the institution's multiple interests, issues, and stakeholders.

The president should possess institution-wide perspective. From this vantage point, and with sufficient authority to back up this significant responsibility, it is the president who typically initiates campuswide reform. In my 1993 survey of strategic planning in higher education at 1,184 colleges and universities, the president was identified by respondents as most critical to overall institutional planning in three ways: as having overall responsibility for planning, as the most likely person to whom chief planning officers reported, and as the most significant driving force behind institutional planning efforts (Dickeson, 1994).

It has become commonplace in the literature about higher education to assert that significant change is much less likely to occur without the active support and approval of the top executive (McCoy, 1995; Neumann and Larson, 1997). In several campus reform efforts I have advised, the generative force was the president. In both state-supported regional universities and community colleges, a new president with a new agenda for the institution initiated the comprehensive program analysis. Motivation for action may have included the need to change the way an institution was managed, or to stimulate program improvement, or to fulfill the president's vision. The readiness of the campus to undergo this examination and the eventual willingness to support its conclusions were usually seen as part of the new president's honeymoon period.

The Board

The president is not necessarily the sole initiator of needed reform. It can come from the board as well. At one land grant research university, the governing board forced a new strategic planning effort, including academic program prioritization, on what it considered a moribund president who, the board leadership believed, was captive of the faculty union. Needless to report, halfway through the process the president resigned, and the board selected a new campus leader whose declared first duty was to see the process through to completion. The institution is now much stronger as a result. The governing board in a private liberal arts college was the initiator in another instance. Governing board members are increasingly being drawn from among the ranks of corporate leadership, where strategic planning and product evaluation techniques are becoming progressively sophisticated. The chair of this particular college board, a woman with strong corporate credentials, recognized that the incongruence between resources and programs was tearing the institution apart and insisted, to her credit, that there be program reform tied to planning and budgeting.

Governing boards are undergoing significant change in the United States, and nowhere is the difference between public and private institutional governance more obvious than in the makeup, style, and direction of governing boards. Public boards—some elected, some appointed by governors for political and sundry reasons—have historically been seen as leisurely to the point of inertia at worst, or agents of bureaucratic regulation at best. Many public presidents today, however, genuinely fear that board members are being elected and appointed for reasons to satisfy ideologies and agendas potentially inimical to the institution. Operating in many states, system boards also are taking on more controversial issues and reform agendas as a more activist model is emerging (Mingle, 1998). Some public board members see themselves as watchdogs, much as if they were appointed to move onto the board and clean things up.

I have chaired the cabinets of governors in two states and have worked with several other governors. Governors see time as extraordinarily precious; they have a short period in which to make an impact. Often in making political appointments to any state board or commission, the governor seeks appointees who will be the eyes and ears of the governor, or to push on behalf of gubernatorial interests while superintending a state department or institution. One governor, upset with the quality of public institutions in his state, appointed a predominance of graduates of elite private institutions to the public higher education boards, hoping that some of what he presumed to be superior quality would rub off on the state's institutions.

What can sometimes result is an academic standoff, with public college administrations hoping to stave off, or outlast, perceived intrusion by board members. When board members are seen as nettlesome outsiders, the opportunities for building needed trust are severely limited. National efforts are under way to improve the selection of public boards, which, although there are fewer of them, oversee institutions enrolling a majority of America's college and university students. The Association of Governing Boards of Universities and Colleges has taken on a multiple-step agenda to secure reforms for public boards, including the expansion of board membership, the merit selection of trustees, and the reduction of sunshine laws (Ingram, 1997).

Private boards, by contrast, tend to self-select members whose commitment to the institution and its continued vitality is evident in a number of ways. Private board members contribute financially to their institutions and ask others to do so. They tend to take longer-term views of the institution and its strategic direction. And they grant significant deference to the chair of the board to represent the board publicly and work closely on its behalf with the president of the institution. This special relationship between the board chair and the president provides a needed link for effective communication that is unusual, if not nonexistent, for their public college counterparts. Although there are exceptions, the rule is that private college board members tend to share their grievances in private. It is also an informal but demonstrable rule that the more publicized a public college board meeting is, the greater is the preening and political posturing tendencies of its members.

Academic program prioritization is serious business. And its careful facilitation requires both an atmosphere conducive to the best interests of the institution and a commitment to see through to completion the decisions that the process will generate. Governing boards may initiate change in some instances, but in all instances they will be required to act with the finality that only their authority permits.

The Provost

As presidents become more and more external officers, raising funds or courting appropriations, academic vice presidents become increasingly the internal leaders of the nation's campuses. In almost every private university where I have aided a prioritization process, the generative impetus for reform was the academic vice president, or provost. Good provosts see connections. And what they see causes them alarm: programs without adequate resources to deliver expected results, competing demands for scarce resources where no demand really wins, duplication of effort and examples of deadwood, and most clearly, uneven levels of quality. In many cases, academic vice presidents have emerged through the ranks of the faculty, and it is to those ranks that they will likely return. Contemplation of life after the vice presidency has often deterred some such leaders from real action. Some provosts may even be jockeying for presidencies of their own. Yet a surprising number have used the opportunity of their vantage point and their power to initiate needed reform to strengthen their institutions.

Leadership and Courage

It is one thing to initiate change; it is quite another to complete it. Before an institution seriously considers undergoing a comprehensive prioritization of academic programs, an old-fashioned "gut check" is necessary: Do we have the leadership, the courage, and the will to see this important task through to completion? Are the leaders, particularly the president, willing to invest political capital in meaningful reform? This review of an institutional profile in courage is necessary in the light of the examples where the will was found wanting and the process failed.

Decision making on a college campus is often political. As in all other legislative arenas, interests collide, and dominant interests—or coalitions of views requisite to securing approval—win out. What is more, the interests do not usually go away after a decision is made. In a legislature, a proposed change in a law will bring to the surface the attention of those who are for or against the change. It is widely accepted that the forces that create a political equilibrium are continuing forces and must be reckoned with in planning for change.

Higher education has produced some spectacular examples of institutional cowardice in the fulfillment of necessary but unpopular reform. One example attracted national attention a decade ago. With the support of her academic vice chancellor, a courageous chancellor of a land grant university instituted a comprehensive program review. The board was on record as supporting this needed renovation. However, as the recommendations moved forward, based on the analysis, faculty members in the affected programs began a statewide lobbying campaign that would be the envy of any political action committee. They contacted legislators, fed misinformation to the media, used students as foils to protest the changes, initiated letter-writing campaigns to special interest groups, inserted anonymous messages in campus mail, and issued threats. All of the pressure was directed at the university's governing board, which, to its discredit, permitted itself to be directly lobbied by faculty in contravention of its own rules about communication channels. The board caved. Allowing political pressure to obscure its own vision of the need for reform, the board halted the reform process, and the dissidents claimed victory for the status quo. The chancellor, frustrated by the hypocrisy of the board that had hired her to conduct the very process they had now rescinded, eventually left to head a more honorable university.

I have worked with governing boards where there was unanimity at the outset about the need for making difficult decisions associated with resource reallocation. But when the going got tough and the lobbying got tougher still, board members abandoned both their principles and their president. In still other instances, boards have split into opposing camps, forcing the administration to negotiate a settlement on issues of academic importance to the institution. As a consultant at one university, I was forced to meet separately with two board factions—one at a downtown restaurant, the other on the campus—in an attempt to foster communication.

This behavior is not only reprehensible; it is preventable. Prior to undertaking academic reform, a clear understanding of its likely controversy should be revealed to and discussed by the board. Legal, financial, and reputational issues will be at stake, as well as academic and management ones. Departments that "own" programs do not readily give them up without a fight. Tactics often include end runs to the board. To the degree that the board has permitted—even encouraged—ex parte communication with faculty, the role and success of the president is jeopardized.

Any number of reform efforts are delayed because the president may be undergoing a performance evaluation by the board. Presidents typically are politically astute. They know that a fractious faculty, upset over program reform, will not likely grade presidential performance favorably. Presidents thus have to strike a balance between their convictions to do what is right and their survivability, without which they get to do nothing at all. "I'm not sure the board will back me" has forestalled more serious reforms than any other single factor.

The board has an anomalous situation to confront in this matter. On the one hand, it is pledged to support the president and his or her administrative team. After all, the primary duty of the board is the selection, support, or removal of the president. On the other hand, a good board member wants to know what is really going on at the institution. It is the fiduciary duty of the board to protect the institution from a president who may be leading it in the wrong direction, for example. It is the institution, after all, to whom the duty is owed, not any particular person in it. But how a board reconciles this anomaly is critical. An appropriate balance between enthusiastic support and healthy skepticism is required.

The problem is compounded because boards are necessarily part time. They typically are composed of individuals busy with other duties and responsibilities—jobs, families, and other interests. Communication is difficult. Bringing a board up to speed on the latest developments on campus is a major task. Boards often lack context. The role usually falls to the president to convey both information and context, and the president already has inordinate demands on her or his time. Among alternative models, one that appears to be successful comes from a regional public university where it is the task of a vice president, who also serves as the secretary of the board, to call each board member at least once a month, merely to keep in touch. This effort, which helps develop context, also permits the surfacing of issues brewing in the mind of the board member, allows the sharing of information, and occasionally results in communicating to the board those concerns of the president that the chief executive might find awkward to bring up personally. Still other presidents will guard jealously the prerogative of direct board communication as their sole responsibility.

Private institutions tend to accomplish this communication function through the chair of the board or an executive committee and with greater frequency. At one private university I advised, the president and the board chair enjoyed an extraordinarily close professional relationship that included daily contact. This level of trust benefited the institution. Perhaps it is the size of private boards— typically over twenty members—that brings about the deference to the chair. Of course, when the communication breaks down between the chair and the rest of the board who do not feel adequately informed, problems arise. These issues about communication and context become increasingly poignant when the institution is undergoing significant change.

Key Questions to Ask

Even before the first program is analyzed or the first database tapped, it is essential for a serious and honest appraisal of important questions:

1. Where is the leadership for this initiative going to come from? Beyond the president and academic vice president, who has the institution-wide perspective to see the need? The vision to focus on the horizon? The capability to inspire others? The capacity to fill the multiple roles that leadership implies? Who are the best change facilitators?

2. Change requires the performance of various functions, and no one person can excel at all of them. Who will take on these component tasks?

   Sanctioning change

   Providing needed resources

   Coaching on technical matters

   Monitoring progress and evaluating results

   Training others on new systems

   Reinforcing positive behaviors

   Encouraging action

   Ensuring effective communication

   Approving adaptations

3. Reform of this type requires extraordinary communication. What will we do differently about the way we communicate this process?

4. Who will be affected by our decisions, and how do they get enfranchised into the process?

5. Besides focusing on innovation, how can we concentrate more on eventual implementation?

6. Is the board on board?

7. How can we ensure that the change we seek will be fully implemented and endure?

Honest answers to these questions before proceeding with academic program prioritization will raise significant issues such as trust, openness, candor, and honor. Academic reform often brings with it controversy, and controversy tests integrity. Among the stakeholders in the ensuing process—students, faculty members, presidents, vice presidents, board members, alumni—are people who care deeply about the institution and believe to varying degrees that its future has been entrusted to their care. The importance of securing commitments of courage in advance is a prerequisite to a successful conclusion.

The unifying force for stakeholders—the flag around which all should rally—is the mission of the institution. The next chapter explains how clarification of what the institution is to do and whom it is to serve is another critical prerequisite for prioritization.

Chapter Three

Reaffirming Institutional Mission

Most institutions can no longer afford to be what
they've become.

The mission of the institution is the academic grid against which
all evaluation of programs must be measured. It is therefore vital
that the mission be reexamined in some cases, revised in other
cases, and reaffirmed in all cases.

Seeking Clarity

In a quest for tighter focus, a limitless mission is of minimal use in
a time of imposing limits. Yet mission statements in higher education are notoriously overbroad. Leslie and Fretwell (1996) observed
that "no question is too small or too large or too challenging to be
contemplated at one institution or another" (p. 83).

Speaking in lofty terms about the discovery and transmission of
knowledge, the value of wisdom, and the regard for the individual,
mission statements typically lack sufficient clarity to articulate to
audiences, internal and external, specific understanding about the
institution, its purposes, or its future. The reasons for this lack of
clarity and specificity are understandable.

Vague Language

Mission statements are typically written in language vague and
timeless enough to appeal to the ages, to cover all eventualities,

29

and to serve in as overarching a stretch as possible. This limitless dimension is designed to cover whatever new notion or program may emerge in the future, and in a time of rapid change, a generalized mission affords protection against the unforeseeable. By so doing, it also protects against certainty.

Political Considerations

Mission statements are usually written by committees. Anyone who has served on such groups knows the process: draft upon draft becomes subjected to revision; arguments ensue about emphasis; debates rage over word choice. The eventual statement takes on a life representative of the values, forces, and compromises that created it. Thus the statement usually reflects the culture (or cultures) of the institution. William Bergquist (1992) has identified four such cultures at colleges and universities: collegial, managerial, developmental, and negotiating. My reading of hundreds of mission statements convinces me that they tend to reflect an accommodation of contradictory cultures, all of which may be present, to varying extents, at a single institution.

Similarly, because the mission must be sold to others, it is written with an eye toward achieving optimum consensus among campus constituencies, particularly faculty. Concepts often emerge with the very pragmatic purpose of securing the political support necessary for its adoption.

Accreditation

One practical application of the mission statement surfaces when it is periodically taken from the institutional shelf and dusted off for decennial accreditation visits. This practice provides another test of its timelessness. Beginning about three decades ago, regional accreditation bodies started to shift emphasis away from evaluating so-called objective or normative measures of quality of institutions; reviewers instead emphasized the degree to which a school achieved its own mission. As accreditation thus became less focused in its prescriptions, mission statements became more blurred.

Changing Purposes

To be fair, many colleges and universities are in transition. Accurate statements about mission are difficult to capture simply because the mission is changing. Institutions have aspirations, and some are in the process of "maturing" into their ambition. Still other colleges have purchased a gown that is overlarge by several sizes, and they are trying to grow into it. Some mission statements strain credulity and bear scant resemblance to what really happens at the place.

Finally, mission statements may include information about purpose that is statutory in origin. Such is true for some public institutions. Some private colleges may secure their purpose from ecclesiastic sources. The purpose of the institution may also reflect a reconciliation between two philosophically competing frameworks: one, that the place exists to accomplish goals; the other, that it exists to serve human needs (Bergquist, 1992, pp. 220–223).

Unique Role and Scope

Ideally a mission statement would address the unique role and scope of the institution. Of the 3,706 not-for-profit colleges and universities in the United States, probably no two are alike. This diversity is both a strength of the American system and a challenge for those who would try to categorize colleges into types. The classification system most commonly referenced is that offered by the Carnegie Foundation for the Advancement of Teaching. Dividing American campuses into several categories (Research I and Liberal Arts II, for example), Carnegie focuses on certain characteristics: admissions selectivity, level of degrees offered and awarded, range and type of programs offered, priority given to research, and federal research dollars generated. This system has spawned an unfortunate and unintended result: the appearance of an academic pecking order, with Research I universities at the top. Seeking to emulate the characteristics of research institutions (for reasons that have more to do with prestige and image than reality) has been a major factor in the serious incongruence in faculty reward structures. Faculty are bright people; they know how to respond to an institution's real incentives.

The Taxonomy of Postsecondary Education Institutions is the product of the National Center for Educational Statistics. Classification of institutions into five broad categories—Major Doctoral-Granting; Comprehensive; General Baccalaureate; Professional and Specialized; and Two-Year Institutions—is made on the basis of level of activity, degrees awarded, breadth and depth of program offerings, and other characteristics.

Researchers have recently approached institutional classification through increasingly sophisticated means. David D. Dill (1997), for example, has analyzed competitive differences among institutions according to their respective environments and task complexity.

Recently the popular press has tried to impose categorization or ranking systems for the ostensible purpose of better public understanding (or to sell magazines that publish the rankings). It is interesting to note that such attempts to rank colleges are decried by those institutions that did not fare well and reprinted for marketing purposes by those that did.

Fundamental Tensions

The role and scope of a single institution remain the prerogative of the institution itself. And as it undertakes the challenge of reaffirming its mission, it will have to cope with five fundamental tensions.

First among these is the *power of its legacy*. As one of the oldest institutions in Western civilization, the university is not noted for radical change. Adherence to the principles that secured the institution's survival is not likely to dissipate easily or readily. As change confronts the campus, reluctance to embrace it is rooted in the fear that what is given up may perhaps be the very linchpin that holds the place together. Arguments for change are met with equal vigor by reminders of the stability and continuity that come with tradition. The force of legacy is usually accompanied by distaste for business concepts or idioms being used to describe campus phenomena. *Marketing, product,* and *customer,* for example, are still unwelcome terms on some parts of the campus.

Second, *the realities of the marketplace will force differentiation.* To the student prospect, all campuses sound alike. As colleges become more aware of the power of consumer sovereignty and learn from marketing experts that product differentiation is essential, pressures increase to appeal to a potential market niche. College admissions recruiting *is* akin to marketing, and colleges that fail to grasp this concept do so at their peril. Market segmentation and competitor analysis are required for survival, as difficult as it will be for those concepts to be uniformly accepted across the institution. As colleges and universities have adopted strategic planning in the recent past, examining the forces external to the institution as well as its internal strengths and weaknesses, an outside-in dimension has been added to academic planning. George Keller's influential book, *Academic Strategy,* written in 1983, persuaded an entire generation of presidents and provosts to differentiate their campuses from the rank and file. The most popular education book in its decade, it taught academic leaders to focus on environmental factors that affected their institutions' futures.

Third, *the campus must wrestle with its true quest for excellence.* While quality is given enormous lip-service at colleges today, the pressures to conform, inflate grades, and retain both students and programs unworthy of higher education persist. On the other hand, I am regularly impressed with the pockets of true quality that exist on every campus. Some programs emerge over time as peaks of quality atop the academic landscape. In every case, some university departments hold to stronger standards of excellence than the institution apparently expects across the board. Often in spite of the prevailing environment around them, a group of scholars will insist on standards of excellence for their students and themselves. They are the departments that recommend only the best of their colleagues for promotion and tenure (as opposed to the many units that send up everybody, with the hope that a higher level in the approval process will "catch" the miscreant who is being advanced). They are the departments that resist the political temptation to look the other way when colleagues fail to deliver quality in teaching, advising, or research. From an institutional perspective, there are never enough strong faculty with the burning need to be the best. But those who are will insist that the institution emphasize excellence as the defining characteristic of its mission. John W. Gardner, whose book on excellence and equality remains the best work on the subject to date, emphasized excellence *and* diversity in colleges:

> We do not want all institutions to be alike. We want institutions to develop their individualities and to keep those individualities. None must be ashamed of its distinctive features so long as it is doing something that contributes importantly to the total pattern, and so long as it is striving for excellence in performance. The highly selective, small liberal arts college should not be afraid to remain small. The large urban institution should not be ashamed that it is large. The technical institute should not be apologetic about being a technical institute. Each institution should pride itself on the role that it has chosen to play and on the special contribution which it brings to the total pattern of American higher education [Gardner, 1961, p. 83].

A fourth dimension will be the *local reconciliation of higher education's functions*. The three-legged stool (teaching, research, and service) creates an imperative for artful balance. It is generally conceded that today's institutions should be shifting relative attention away from research, except, of course, for the 239 institutions where significant research or doctoral-level program preeminence is a clear expectation. The greater focus is on teaching—or, more accurately, the facilitation of learning. The age-old conflict among these three functions continues today because each is essential for the full fruition of higher education's promise. The reconciliation is more than a battle over scarce resources. It is a battle over values. Higher educators would do well to recognize that the dilemma about functions is identical in form to that experienced by other multiple-purpose organizations. Churches rage over worship versus outreach versus missions. Hospitals argue about balance among patient care and research and education. It is this multiple functionality that adds to the confoundment of noneducators as they try to understand, much less solve, higher education's problems. But an institution must reconcile and then declare the relative weight it wishes to place on each function. In the absence of such a declaration, the institution will continue to be buffeted by uncertainty about who it is and what it stands for.

Finally, I would ask institutions to *enunciate in their mission statements the specific ways they fulfill their most essential purposes*.

Community Colleges

For the great majority of community colleges, the prevailing wisdom would spell out five such purposes (Doucette and Hughes, 1990):

1. The transfer mission: Preparing students to transfer to four-year colleges and universities
2. The career preparation mission: Preparing students for new careers, career change, and career advancement
3. The developmental education mission: Expanding higher education opportunities to populations previously unserved
4. The continuing education and community service mission: Serving the expressed economic development needs of college constituents and communities

5. The access mission: Providing for universal access to higher education

Traditional Colleges and Universities

Four-year colleges and universities with a liberal arts tradition generally espouse five purposes, but should spell out with greater precision the extent to which they intend to accomplish them.

Preparing Students for Careers. Nationally nearly 80 percent of incoming college freshmen list as the most important reason for going to college "to be able to get a better job" (Astin, 1998). Aware of this marketing demographic, institutions have responded with an academic smorgasbord of career and professional programs to entice students to enroll. These programs are typically added on to the liberal arts curriculum base. My analysis of the intended majors identified by incoming freshmen for a recent report year (1997) revealed that 64.2 percent of new students intended to major in professional, career, or work-related fields; 27.6 percent in traditional liberal arts and sciences; and 8.2 percent confessed they were undecided (Dickeson, 1997).

Transmitting the Civilization. In the medieval university, the civilization was transmitted through the *trivium*—grammar, rhetoric, and logic—and the *quadrivium*—arithmetic, geometry, astronomy, and music. Today's student has it a little tougher. The curriculum at most institutions encompasses dozens and often hundreds of degree programs accomplished through hundreds and often thousands of courses. Harold Enarson once referred to this as that "non-mosaic of requirements and electives we call the curriculum" (1990, p. 1A). In part, this evolution came about because the curriculum in higher education has become more fragmented; finding any meaning in the whole consequently becomes increasingly difficult. In part, however, it is because the civilization that is to be transmitted has become increasingly complex. Institutions have obligations to see that students' degree and course choices lead them down paths that will give them the greatest meaning. Integrity and coherence of curriculum will be the keys to fulfilling these obligations. Many institutions seek to redress incoherence through a core curriculum.

Teaching How to Think. Futurists predict that the average worker will change jobs four times and careers twice. The odds are that today's incoming freshman will be employed a few years after graduation at a job that does not exist today. Half of all the jobs existing today did not exist twenty years ago. Aristotle observed that the purpose of education is to train the mind to think, regardless of what it is thinking about. The current emphasis among liberal arts advocates—to strengthen our understanding of critical thinking—is born of this essential purpose. The acquisition of thinking skills thus depends not on what the mind knows but on how it evaluates any new fact or argument. Since change is the most likely constant today's students will face, thinking will be the way they will adapt and cope and survive and flourish.

Liberating the Individual. Through education students are no longer bound by past prejudices or superstitions. Graduates should view who they are and how they fit into this world in changed ways. Their views of races, genders, and cultures other than their own should have changed. (This liberation is the real reason for embracing diversity in admissions practices, not merely to comply with an executive order.) Preparing students for an uncertain world includes preparing them for the millions of ideas that have not been thought of yet. In their lifetimes, graduates will need to be liberated through their education to imagine discoveries as yet unimagined.

Teaching Values. The fully educated person understands and acts on the moral and ethical components of life. As we know from so many historic examples, it is not the knowledge one gains from an education but the use of it that is more important. This is where institutions that still embrace the religious traditions on which they were founded have it all over other colleges and universities. But the reawakening of programs in ethics—particularly tied to career programs, ironically—is a harbinger that even public institutions recognize that one's education is incomplete without comprehension of the concomitant values, commitments, obligations, and convictions that accompany an intellectual base.

Research Universities

For research universities, the imperative is to add to as well as draw from the fund of knowledge. This mission is buttressed by significant increases in external support for research dollars, new partnerships with business and industry to help solve some of society's most pressing problems, and new calls for involving students in hands-on research at ever earlier stages in their education. America's higher education research engine is the hallmark of its preeminence in the world. Scholarship is valued in part because of the reputational dimensions of the academy and in part because it is more easily measurable than either teaching or service.

New Ways to Look at Mission

As institutions reexamine their essential purposes, opportunities emerge to view campus processes and results through different lenses. Here are three significant trends that colleges and universities would do well to accommodate in their mission self-appraisal.

New Emphasis on Learning

Research institutions are feeling enormous pressures to shift the pendulum toward teaching the undergraduate student and a corresponding pressure at nonresearch institutions to get back to the teaching business. This recalibration in academic attitude has resulted in—and in some sense been driven by—new definitions of scholarship (Boyer, 1990) and calls for reaffirmation of historic purposes. A recent example of such a report was released by the Kellogg Commission on the Future of State and Land-Grant Universities, authored by twenty-five current or former presidents of such institutions (Kellogg Commission, 1997). First among its recommendations for academic reform is the principle that the university should be a "learning community": "This university defines itself as a learning community, one that supports and inspires academic growth and learning among faculty, staff, students, and learners of all kinds, on-campus and off. Learning serves all of them; and all of them serve learning. Oriented around learners' needs, this university is committed to maintaining a first-rate environment for learning" (Kellogg Commission, 1997, p. 21).

Focusing on Benefits

An additional approach to looking at institutional mission through external lenses is to assess the degree to which the mission reflects the commonly identified benefits of higher education. In 1998 the Institute for Higher Education Policy conducted a study, underwritten by the Ford Foundation and The Education Resources Institute, on the combination of benefits accruing to individuals and society from higher education (*Reaping the Benefits*, 1998):

- Public economic benefits, such as increased tax revenues, greater productivity, increased consumption, increased workforce flexibility, and decreased reliance on government financial support
- Private economic benefits, such as higher salaries and benefits, employment, higher savings levels, improved working conditions, and personal and professional mobility
- Public social benefits, such as reduced crime rates, increased charitable giving and community service, increased quality of civic life, social cohesion and appreciation of diversity, and improved ability to adapt to and use technology

- Private social benefits, including improved health and life expectancy, improved quality of life for offspring, better consumer decision making, increased personal status, and more hobbies and leisure

The primary purpose of the benefits study was to assist public policymakers in understanding the payoffs for public support of higher education. But the results may also serve as a possible framework for analysis of institutional mission. The question a campus might ask in such a self-examination is this: How do our purposes, functions, values, and programs comport with higher education's benefits?

Focusing on Competencies

Finally, a mission reaffirmation may want to include responding to the competency-based education movement. In general terms, Evers, Rush, and Berdrow (1998) have identified four major domains that college graduates need proficiency in: base competencies (such as mobilizing innovation and change, managing people and tasks, communicating, and managing self); general knowledge and values to understand the world; specific skills in an area of expertise; and specific knowledge in an area of "knowledge that is transient."

The competency-based movement is likely to grow, as employers make increasing demands on institutions to deliver graduates more readily able to work. Its real expansion, however, will likely come as the distance-learning industry coalesces around competency-based education as its academic medium of exchange (as contrasted with the traditional transcript, for example) for the future.

The Need for Reaffirmation

The importance of reaffirming mission prior to undertaking comprehensive program reform should be evident. If the mission is unrealistically overbroad, then the claim of meeting the criterion of "centrality to mission" is perforce applicable to any academic program. If the mission is based on assumptions that are no longer valid or, worse, does not contemplate new assumptions about the realities confronting the institution, a program prioritization may become skewed. Examples of such assumptions include the following:

- Expectations placed on the institution by its key constituencies, which may have shifted
- Characteristics of its student profile, which no doubt have changed to require more emphasis than in the past on remedial education (McGrath and Townsend, 1997)
- Changes in laws and regulations affecting program delivery, such as provision for disabled students (Barnett and Li, 1997)
- Innovations in technology that have altered our thinking about such things as asynchronous learning and information infrastructure (Dolence and Norris, 1995)
- Current data on what competitive institutions are up to

In sum, a reaffirmed mission is inextricably linked to a solid and dynamic strategic plan. And as such, the mission should be periodically revisited as part of the planning process.

In a time when campuses are overprogrammed for the resources they enjoy, the focus of the college or university should be tightened. Its role and mission should permit only those activities that need to be done and that the institution and its people do well. The mission, a synthesis of the college's functions, purposes, and values, should summon the institution to its future, not its past. It should resolve conflicts over what the college does, why it exists, and whom it serves. It should take into account the likely forces that will affect its students' lives in the future.

Institutions seeking transformation are being weighed down by a plethora of programs that to some extent represent commitments to the past. What will be required is a balance between continuity and stability on the one hand, and responsiveness and flexibility on the other. The importance of this task cannot be overestimated. A renewed mission creates, among other things, the opportunity to recalibrate the proper range and mix of all the institution's programs.

Chapter Four

Defining What Constitutes a Program

If you believe in reincarnation, come back as an
academic program and enjoy eternal life.

Most colleges and universities will be amazed when they realize the number of programs they have accumulated. Counting both academic and nonacademic programs, it is not unusual to find hundreds of programs, and in the case of larger institutions, thousands.

Program proliferation mirrors the national academic landscape, where it is probably impossible to know the total number of programs available in the United States. The U.S. Department of Education conducts regular statistical analysis on students graduating from program categories: 102 certificate and associate degree program categories and 104 bachelor's and postbaccalaureate degree program categories (Clery, Lee, and Knapp, 1998).

The popularity of academic programs shifts over time, and it is interesting to track the changes. Subject matter interest is reflective of societal and economic shifts. Certain fields in agriculture, for example, will not graduate a single student in the country in a given year, while popular majors like business management will yield a quarter-million graduates. Academic program proliferation is seen in the published guidebooks available to students. *Barron's Profiles of American Colleges*, for example, lists approximately 670 different undergraduate degree programs at 1,640 accredited four-year colleges in the United States (*Barron's Profiles*, 1997). And at the graduate level, it takes the Educational Testing Service four volumes to list the certificate, master's, professional, specialist, and doctoral degree programs available: 3,960 of them at 865 accredited institutions in the United States and Canada (*The Official Directory of Graduate Programs*, 1997).

In the arena of nonacademic programs, no national data are available to identify the burgeoning growth of institutional responsibilities. Writing nearly thirty years ago, JB Lon Hefferlin observed that "the modern American multiversities have grown by absorbing one by one the multitude of services formerly performed by specialized institutions. They have grafted onto the undergraduate college the forms and functions of the technical institute, the graduate school, the research bureau, the independent professional school, the experiment station, the Chautauqua, lyceum, correspondence school, boarding house, finishing school, encounter group and museum" (Hefferlin, 1969, p. 31).

Nothing in the intervening decades has abated that trend. Janet Donald identifies this phenomenon as the "criterion of exclusive competence." Can some other social agency respond to a problem, or is only the university equipped to deal with it (Donald, 1997, p. 15)?

The historic tendency has been to add and not to delete, to plant and not to prune. As the collegiate institution confronts the realities of prioritizing, it must first inventory, and then evaluate simultaneously, all its programs.

What Constitutes a Program?

An operational definition of a program is any activity or collection of activities of the institution that consumes resources (dollars, people, space, equipment, time). Examples abound: the bachelor's degree program in biology, the office for international students, the research institute on aging. Over time, institutions have created programs to fulfill special felt needs of a particular time or for a special audience, allocated resources to the programs, and permitted the programs to become considered a continuing part of the institution's plans, budgets, and obligations.

Programs, Not Departments

It is important early on to distinguish between a *program* and the *department* that offers it. Programs are more usually narrow and disciplinary in nature. In the academic world, programs typically fall within an academic content discipline—the minor in chemistry, an area of concentration in political science, a speech and hearing clinic—and the providers usually train in and identify with the specific discipline. A department, by contrast, is an administrative unit of the institution, designated to manage the resources associated with the programs under its jurisdiction. A department manages several programs. In larger institutions where there are more ample resources, the trend has been to create and sustain a department as an administrative unit that focuses solely on one discipline and its programs. Small and medium-sized colleges, however, cannot afford that. Programs in psychology and sociology at a smaller institution might be administered by a department of social sciences, where at a larger university each discipline might have its own department.

At most institutions, the faculty in a discipline lust after sole departmental status, despite the lack of resources to justify the separate administrative structure and its attendant costs. The argument used to aspire to separate departmental status—that *other* disciplines have separate departments—is another example of egalitarianism on campus. In a time of scarce resources, however, *program* and *department* should not be considered synonymous.

Discrete Programs

The definition of program should include all programs using the institution's total resources. Stated another way, all resources should be allocated to one or more programs. And the definition should be discrete enough to permit real analysis to take place. As an example, at a major state university that took on the prioritization process, the department of biology was found to engage in eleven different programs:

1. Bachelor of Science, general biology major
2. Bachelor of Science in Biology, botany emphasis
3. Bachelor of Science in Biology, zoology emphasis
4. Biology, baccalaureate minor
5. Biology, general education courses for other majors
6. Biology, service courses to other undergraduate programs
7. Master of Science, botany
8. Master of Science, zoology
9. Doctor of Philosophy, multiple emphases within biology
10. Biology, service courses needed by other graduate and professional programs
11. Biology, research institute in specialized area.

These eleven programs obviously shared common resources, notably faculty, who might teach sections of courses in several of the programs over the period of a year. Laboratories and computer facilities typically are also seen as property of the department, even though multiple programs make use of them. By analyzing what takes place on the campus by program, decisions about priorities can be informed with greater precision. A review simply of the biology department, without disaggregating its program components, would have yielded insufficient understanding of the multiple expectations being placed on this important part of the institution's offerings.

Multiple Expectations of Programs

Programs at most institutions fulfill many needs. A major in a subject matter is typically composed of more courses offered outside the subject than in it. Generally a third of a student's undergraduate degree is composed of courses required for the major, a third in general or liberal studies, and the remaining third in a minor and electives. There are obvious exceptions. Several professional degrees at the baccalaureate level (engineering, for example) may require heavier emphasis and more time spent on the major, at the cost of exposing the student to other subjects of interest and fields of academic inquiry. But in all cases, students will require courses in subject matter outside the narrow discipline. Engineers require advanced courses in mathematics. Nurses must take course work in biology and chemistry. Psychology majors should study human anatomy and physiology. Future teachers should spend most of their academic time in the liberal arts and sciences. A degree program is thus composed of courses offered by the subject specialty *and* by such "service" courses (those required to be taken from other offering areas).

In addition, most undergraduate degree programs require a substantial exposure to general or liberal education courses, also presumably taken outside the content specialty. Some campuses design and offer courses that may be taken solely for general or liberal education credit, thus ensuring philosophic cohesion. But for most other colleges, the general education program consists of a cafeteria of course choices and a requirement to graze, in a distributed fashion, among the major intellectual food groups. In some instances courses perform multiple duties: they may be taken for general education credit, or they may even count for major, minor, or other purposes (Gaff and others, 1997).

The point is that a subject discipline may be engaged in multiple programs because it seeks to meet multiple expectations. The discipline simultaneously offers majors, minors, service courses, and general education courses, and no analysis of that area would be complete without identifying the sum of the contributions it is making to—and the resources it is drawing from—the whole.

Several years ago the National Center for Higher Education Management Systems developed a sophisticated tool for analyzing the contributing components of a degree program, recognizing the importance of this set of academic interrelationships. Called the Induced Course Load Matrix, the system graphically displays the interaction among the many disciplines that constitute a typical degree program. The concept has found its way into several formulas for planning and budgeting in higher education. Whether a campus uses this particular tool or not, the concept of interrelatedness is crucial to an understanding of academic articulation and coherence.

Distinguishing *Prioritization* from *Review*

Some institutions may argue that they are exempt from the kind of academic program prioritization being recommended here because they conduct periodic "program reviews." Program review has been in vogue in higher education for many years and is proving to be a useful means of academic management (Barak and Breier, 1990; Mets, 1997). But its value is limited and can be distinguished from academic program prioritization in several ways.

First, the review process usually involves a departmental self-study, which seeks to assess its own strengths and weaknesses and may be aided, in the best instances, by external peer review. The underlying assumptions are that the program or department will continue in operation and that it does not compete with other departments or programs for the institution's scarce resources. Neither assumption should be valid today.

Research into program review also reveals that it is used primarily for program improvement and that it is often not tied effectively to resource allocation (Barak and Sweeney, 1995; Farmer and Napieralski, 1997). This inadequacy means that the recommendations that come from the program review usually are not fully acted on by the administration, because resources are insufficient. Resources are insufficient because they are being consumed by other programs, some of which may be of lesser value to the institution and its future. That is why reallocation, based on prioritization, is necessary.

A final distinguishing characteristic of reviews is that *all* programs, not a chosen few, should be assessed, and assessed *simultaneously*, for effective comparison and prioritization to be accomplished.

The wisdom of this approach was brought home to me in a discussion with a campus provost. He proudly reported to me that his university's program review policy required a rigorous analysis of six departments annually. Based on the fact that the institution conducted over six hundred programs, a thoroughgoing analysis would thus have required one hundred years to accomplish.

Nonacademic Programs

Although the primary focus of this book is academic programs, nonacademic programs should also be subject to review, analysis, and prioritization. Again, a department or division may be the administrative unit that maintains responsibility for a number of programs. The physical plant department may house four programs: maintenance of buildings, management of utilities, preventive maintenance, and new construction. For legal or bonding reasons, public institutions may separate these four programs into publicly funded or auxiliary funded sources so as to account for programs appropriately.

A growing area of the higher education enterprise is related to student affairs and student development functions. These programs (for that is what they are) may be found in most campus settings, yet their administrative home may be subsumed under one or more major divisions of an institution, usually headed by a vice president.

Exhibit 4.1 is a matrix of twenty-three such programs and the possible locations where they may be found in most institutions. Although one would expect that all these programs are administratively housed under the rubric of "Student Affairs" or "Student Life," the reality in practice confirms that any of these programs can report to any institutional division. Larger institutions have developed variations on or subsets of these twenty-three basic programs, and some mount dozens of additional programs designed to assist students in nonacademic, or cocurricular ways. The learning benefits of many such programs are well established (Donald, 1997).

Exhibit 4.1. Student Affairs Functions.

Abbreviations for possible location: AA = Academic Affairs; SL = Student Life; AD = Administration; UA = University Advancement

Function	Possible Location			
	AA	SL	AD	UA
Financial aid programs, policies, and administration				
Enrollment management initiatives and research				
Minority student recruitment, retention, and programs				
Campus alcohol, substance abuse, and drug education programs and policies				
Student conduct and discipline codes and procedures; student judicial tribunals				
Student outcomes assessment research and reports				
Child care policies and services				
Student retention programs and research				
Liaison with student government associations and officers				
Liaison with federal agencies on Higher Education Act and other student-related programs				
Student organizations, activities, fraternities and sororities				
Auxiliary operations (food service, bookstore, unions, and so on)				
Residence halls: Facilities, renovations, construction				
Residence halls: Programs, staff, activities				
Cultural diversity initiatives				
Academic support services, advising, skills enhancement				
Athletics, club and intramural sports				
International student programs, immigration regulations				
Student health, counseling, and personal development				
Crisis centers				
Student legal aid				
Disabled student services				
Career planning and placement				

Benefits of Program Analysis

The subdivision of the institution's many activities and enterprises, academic and nonacademic, into discrete programs enables the following work to be done:

- Analysis focused on preselected criteria
- Concentration on resource development and resource utilization, somewhat independent of the vagaries of administrative structure
- Focus on the specific elements that address efficiency, effectiveness, and centrality to mission
- A systematic basis to identify opportunities to increase revenue, reduce costs, improve quality, and strengthen reputation

Once all programs of the institution have been identified, it is time to focus attention on choosing the appropriate standard criteria to be used in measuring them.

Chapter Five

Selecting Appropriate Criteria

Far better an approximate answer to the right
question, which is often vague, than an exact
answer to the wrong question, which can always be
made precise.

—*John Tukey*

Writers on the subject of analyzing academic programs have differed on the number and kinds of criteria to be used (Shirley and Volkwein, 1978; Cope, 1981, 1991; Bergquist and Armstrong, 1986; Skolnik, 1989; Barak and Breier, 1990; Farmer and Napieralski, 1997). From as few as three to as many as seven different criteria have been suggested in the past. Of course, it is the quality and not the quantity of gauges that would yield the most meaningful understanding of relative program worth. My own experience in working with colleges and universities throughout the country has generated a profound appreciation for the multiple and complex ways that academic programs are capable of examination. In higher education we tend to measure the things that are easiest to measure. Costs are readily measurable. FTEs can be counted. Faculty publications are no doubt used to assess tenurability and promotability in part because they are readily quantifiable. At the same time, one often hears that some standards (quality, learning capacity, or something else) are simply not measurable, and thus they are disregarded. This myopia is wrong. The challenge is to begin to assess even the most difficult of criteria, particularly if they are important to a fuller understanding of programs. Instead of accepting "it's difficult to measure" as the conclusion, real creativity among some faculty and staff leaders has emerged to develop increasing levels of sophistication in assessing relative program worth. This chapter is a distillation of that creativity.

To permit a synthesis of quantitative and qualitative indicators that will facilitate meaningful prioritization, I recommend using ten criteria:

1. History, development, and expectations of the program

2. External demand for the program

3. Internal demand for the program

4. Quality of program inputs and processes

5. Quality of program outcomes

6. Size, scope, and productivity of the program

7. Revenue and other resources generated by the program

8. Costs and other expenses associated with the program

9. Impact, justification, and overall essentiality of the program

10. Opportunity analysis of the program

Each of these criteria can be supported by data that, properly cast, generate valuable information. In applying criteria to an analysis of academic programs, several postulates are in order. First, the program analysis that leads to prioritization should be accomplished on an individual campus basis. In a very real sense, an institution's curricular portfolio represents its *academic allocation of values* and is therefore unique to that institution. There are no correct cost figures or appropriate percentages of faculty with doctorates. What may work in one institution may not necessarily be implantable to another, primarily because its mission is different. The college's development, relative adaptation to change, internal strengths and weaknesses, and all its other characteristics are essentially exclusive, although similar to those in other places here and there. Although higher education is highly socialized (conducting fifty-minute classes and using a common lexicon, for examples), significant differences among colleges prevail.

The significant differences among institutional cultures—and the corresponding pitfalls of cross-institutional comparisons—have been well documented (Ewell, 1997a). It is necessary to be informed about how other institutions are conducting programs, but the programs themselves are rarely comparable, and benchmarking is likely to be inexact. Benchmarking—comparing our practices with best practices among peer institutions, for example—is invaluable for program *improvement* purposes, but for *prioritization* purposes, we are comparing internal programs to each other. The program prioritization process should seek to secure a measure of the relative worth of a program as against all other programs at the same institution.

Not all campuses will want to embrace all ten criteria, and not all programs will be able to respond to all the criteria-related questions. But to the extent possible, a more comprehensive approach to analyzing an institution's academic programs will likely yield more defensible and academically worthy decisions. A great deal of information can be generated from this process, and administrators would be wise to envision its subsequent uses.

Getting Started

The purpose of the process that draws on these criteria is to permit full and fair examination of programs. Thus it is important at the outset for the institution to undertake several things.

Announce the criteria in advance.

I strongly recommend using all ten criteria. Prioritization of programs is extraordinarily important to a campus and its people, and due care should be taken to ensure that all relevant information that bears on a program is taken into account in institutional decisions. Programs have multiple facets. As campus practitioners begin to review programs, criterion by criterion, new or fuller information will surface about the program. Higher education is focused—some would say unduly—on process. But by taking the time to secure decisions that are data based and mission driven, the likelihood of acceptance of eventual results is enhanced.

Several campuses with which I have worked on this process have taken shortcuts. Due to the press of financial or other exigencies, and occasionally because insufficient data were available, they have evaluated programs using as few as three of the criteria (typically demand, cost, and quality). And although that approach no doubt met their immediate needs, a comprehensive review might have yielded richer information and presumably better-justified decisions. Campuses that undertook the full analysis instead came away from the process convinced they had made stronger decisions more consonant with their ongoing strategies. But whatever criteria are chosen should be clearly identified in advance and communicated consistently throughout the process.

Involve program faculty and staff in designing additional data formats to fit the criteria.

There are numerous ways to measure a single criterion, and faculty and staff closest to the delivery of the program will think of still other ways. It has been my experience—and I commend it to others—to conduct faculty workshops on campus about the criteria in order to discuss ways in which the criteria might be better measured and solicit additional suggestions for data formats or portfolios of information that might better articulate the nexus between a particular criterion and the program. In every instance, creative ideas surfaced that improved both the perception of the process and the results that followed. Faculty in the programs are not only creative and knowledgeable; they are also heavy stakeholders in a program prioritization process. It should be communicated clearly that the best way to preserve and possibly improve a program is to provide high-quality information to buttress the program's standing. This bottom-up approach places responsibility for championing a program on a basis that is more rational and less reliant on politics as usual.

Decide what relative weights should be given the criteria.

Not all criteria are equal in importance and therefore should not be given equal weight. The relative value of "quality inputs" versus "quality outcomes," for example, would engage the sustained debate of most experts in higher education and elsewhere. "Costs" may hold greater sway at some campuses than "history and development." Each criterion selected presumably has some value in understanding the program and shaping appraisal about it and should thus carry some weight in the analyses and judgments that follow. But it will be for each campus to decide the relative weights.

As is the case with all of these postulates, the intent is to provide a framework for analysis that facilitates, rather than stifles, the prioritization of programs. To be meaningful, the process must be tailored to the uniqueness of each institution. At the same time it is important for each institution to demonstrate its responsibility in highly credible and visible ways that its publics can see and appreciate.

Provide data to support the criteria.

Deciding things based on information requires more data than deciding things based on power. Although many of the criteria selected will require programs and departments to submit information that only they possess, much of the burden of data collection can be relieved by providing it centrally. Larger institutions have institutional research offices with substantive databases required to respond to the myriad of reports expected from them. Such offices can supply information commonly useful for all programs. Smaller campuses may not have as strong an institutional research presence, and culling information from the admissions, registrar, and bursar's offices, or wherever else it may be located, will be required. External sources for comparative information and national demand data, for example, are available. And the growing presence of Internet sources is making information accessible in cheaper, more direct ways.

Note that data do not substitute for sound judgments.

Some campuses overengineer program prioritization. The goal of validity in data presentation and analysis can be taken too far, for example. Statisticians on the faculty or in the institutional research office want to ensure fairness through mathematical modeling or computer simulations of criteria, weights, and statistical tests. Some programs advance information in quantities that suggest they misunderstand the concept of weight. Others will lament the data collection as "paralysis by analysis."

Although the quest for quantification nirvana is understandable, it is unlikely to be achieved in as human an institution as a college or university. Peter Ewell (1997b) calls it "excessive methodological purity" (p. 377). Taken too far, this approach will yield a statistically pure but wholly irrelevant institution as a result. *What is required is judgment.* After all the data are in and the recommendations forwarded, institutional leaders, with institution-wide perspective and responsible for overall stewardship, must make judgments about program configuration. I am unaware of a computer-generated model or academic template that can do the same.

Applying the Criteria

What can we expect to learn about each program by applying these criteria? Following are approximately 150 suggested questions and issues that relate to the ten criteria and can be converted into data formats. If used thoughtfully, the information that emerges can instruct campus decision makers in their quest for sound decisions.

Criterion 1: History, Development, and Expectations of the Program

It is important to know the history and development of a particular program. Why was the program established? What are its academic antecedents? How has the program evolved over the years? What were the institution's original expectations? How have those expectations changed? What were the origins of initial support? What is the degree to which the program has adapted to meet change?

In particular, what is the degree to which the program has adapted to the changing demographic characteristics of the institution's students? Such changes, on a national basis, reveal the following facts about undergraduate students:

- They are more likely to enroll on a part-time than a full-time basis.
- On average, many have family and work responsibilities, as compared to more traditional students.
- They are less likely to be prepared adequately for the rigors of higher education and more likely to need remediation in one or more academic subjects and skills.
- They are less likely to expect to succeed in college, to be adequately motivated to succeed, and therefore less likely to persist.

To the extent that these characteristics are representative of the students coming to this campus, what has the program done to engage these students?

What is the maturity level of the program? Is it a fledgling program, recently authorized and still building toward its initial survival threshold? What progress is it making? Or is it a solid cornerstone of the overall curriculum, fully mature and attracting attention to the institution? What is the overall visibility of the program?

Finally, has the context changed within which the program is expected to operate? Would this program, for example, meet the expectations that the institution now places on new programs up for approval today?

Answers to these questions would inform an analyst about such things as program efficacy. A rating system could be devised, with scores for program maturity, adaptability, and congruence with institutional expectations. Again, the program is not being compared with some abstract ideal but with all other programs on the campus.

Criterion 2: External Demand for the Program

This criterion seeks to assess the need for and attractiveness of the program. It is essentially data driven, using national statistics that are readily available, representing, for example, incoming student interest in programs, at least at the undergraduate freshman level. If it is true that demographics is destiny, then data about demand will presage the viability of academic programs.

For several reasons, care must be taken in relying too heavily on national demand data. Many students change their minds about choice of academic major after a term or two of college. They are exposed to academic programs and choices in college they simply did not know existed when they were in high school completing the surveys on which the national data are based. Too, there is a faddishness about academic major choice that is disquieting. The longer one looks at trend lines, the more peaks and valleys in demand curves one can observe. Teacher education has had its ups and downs over the years. Engineering and business majors fall in and out of favor over time. Changes in academic preference by women have revolutionized disciplines formerly predominated by men. Shortly after the movie *All The President's Men* became popular, there was a glut of would-be journalists. We have surely overfilled the need for psychologists. And so it goes. Although a campus needs to be mindful of demand data, a considered look at trend lines over time is also advisable.

In addition to national demand data for program enrollments, what has been the local demand trend? Looking at enrollments in the program for the past five years would give a sense of direction and at least prompt penetrating questions about the choices students have been making. How is demand being met by competing institutions that offer the same program? Are other institutions in the same enrollment catchment zone experiencing the same kinds of proportionate numbers by program? What is the likely potential for future enrollments—a demonstrated, documentable potential— and are the resources for the program under- or overallocated for the future? Is the program offered at a level that corresponds to the demand? For example, do we need a full-blown baccalaureate program to meet the demand, or will a minor do? Is the demand sufficient to mount (or dispose of) a master's degree in the subject matter? What are the characteristics of patrons, clients, or customers of the program? Will their numbers and interests foretell a continuing need for the program? What other forces are at work in the surrounding environment that affect this program? Do external demands suggest that the institution continue this program? In some public institutions, statutory pressure exists to deliver certain programs, and that certainly constitutes "demand" that an institution would ignore at its peril. In some church-related schools, there is an expectation that certain programs will exist to turn out church leaders, teachers, and choir directors; again, this constitutes a demand that may condition ongoing financial support.

Scoring this criterion is relatively easy. External demand is knowable and calculable. Measuring demand for this program as against all others—and against programs that the institution might be better off to offer—would yield information of value to the prioritization project.

Criterion 3: Internal Demand for the Program

Many academic programs are necessary simply because they are required to support other programs. A high degree of interdependence exists among academic disciplines, especially because programs are designed to develop well-rounded graduates. Some disciplines perform extraordinary service beyond taking care of their own majors and minors and should be given appropriate credit for doing so. It is this internal demand feature that is the focus of this criterion.

Data on internal demand are readily attainable. What are the enrollments in courses required for other programs? What proportion of enrollments are for major, minor, general studies, or service purposes? What programs would suffer, or possibly fail, without the service courses offered by another program? Some programs have a significant presence in the college's general education program—philosophy comes to mind—but might not attract as many majors. To evaluate philosophy—or any other program—solely on the number of its degree candidates would be shortsighted. Still other departments might not pass muster in most criteria but deserve continuation because of the internal demand they generate. One private college discovered such serious shortcomings in the quality of its science program that it initially wanted to cut the program back severely. But looking at the internal demand for science courses generated by popular—and good—allied health programs, officials made a different decision: to beef up the sciences to meet higher expectations.

Are there other internal claims on the program's resources that should be revealed? Does the program produce services needed by other parts of the campus? Looking to the future, is there potential for internal demand because this program may have pioneered new approaches to collaborative learning or uses of technology likely to be emulated by other programs?

Scoring the criterion of internal demand can be accomplished by rating the relative dependence the campus has on this program.

Criterion 4: Quality of Program Inputs and Processes

The tradition in higher education has been to measure quality by assessing inputs: the quality of the faculty, students, facilities, equipment, and other resources necessary to mount a program. This is the tradition of meritocracy. Although there is a decided shift toward

measuring what a campus actually accomplishes with these resources (the outcomes approach seen in Criterion 5), there is little
debate that quality inputs do make a significant difference in sustaining quality. This criterion seeks to address the quality of a program's inputs and evaluate the processes that may be in place to take
advantage of those resources.

The categories of inputs are well established.

Faculty and Staff. This category includes current faculty and
staff profiles and numbers, breadth and depth of program exposure,
and knowledge bases. It looks at the proportion of faculty with ter-
minal degrees appropriate for the field, years of experience in the
discipline, expertise in related fields that bear on the discipline,
scholarly and creative contributions to the discipline, and recognition accorded them. In sum, a program is inextricably connected
with the people who provide it. In terms of credentials, skills, and
capacities, how good are they? How intellectually current? How
available are qualified faculty and staff in this field? If we are to
retain or expand this program, what are the potential personnel
resources in this discipline, the market conditions, the trend lines?
Can we attract and retain the people necessary to make the program successful? How do our faculty and staff stack up against peer
comparator institutions or competitor institutions?

Percentage of Instruction Offered by Full-Time Faculty. The
most serious decline in quality inputs in higher education in the
past twenty-five years has been the increasing overreliance on part-
time faculty. National reports acknowledge that nearly half of
instruction is now provided by part-timers. Although many, if not
most, of these instructors are no doubt well qualified, they cannot
possibly maintain the continuity, stability, and ongoing rigor required of full and active participation in academic planning, programming, advising, scholarship, and service necessary to sustain
academic program preeminence (Finnegan, 1997). This assertion
does not mean that all full-time faculty are good and part-timers are

evil. Indeed, Gappa and Leslie (1993) make a strong case for the increasingly valuable services that part-time faculty and staff bring to the academic table. But the resulting bifurcation of the academy is serious. An institution must maintain appropriate balance between the stability represented by full-time faculty on the one hand and the flexibility offered by employing part-time faculty on the other. Many institutions, however, notably a large proportion of community colleges, have become seriously imbalanced. Flexibility—and lower personnel costs at the price of quality—have tipped the scales in the wrong direction. Student complaints that they are being taught by "rent-a-profs" are valid. Accreditation agencies are rightfully looking into this issue. As a criterion, a program's quality may suffer to the extent that less than full-time human resources increase.

Students. The quality of programs can be measured by the quality of students attracted to them. Programs that are more selective in their admissions practices tend to attract students more likely to persist because they are better prepared and often better motivated to succeed. As the demographics indicate fewer available students with desirable academic profiles, selective programs and selective institutions are having and will continue to have a tougher time of it. Measures include high school grades, rank in class, Advanced Placement scores, transfer transcripts, scores on achievement tests, special experiences that students bring to the program, and other academic results. Nonacademic measures of motivation and retention proneness are harder to come by but are available. The essential question to be answered is: What is the congruence between the students in the program and the likelihood of their being successful?

Curriculum. Is the curriculum of the program appropriate to the breadth, depth, and level of the discipline? How coherent is the curriculum? Is it designed to provide integration, or is the student expected to do the integrating sometime along the senior year? To what degree does the curriculum meet the particular learning needs and styles of the students? How dynamic is it? When was the last reform or overhaul to ensure comprehension of the knowledge explosion? How "internationalized" is the curriculum, that is, how does the curriculum purport to prepare a graduate who will be living and working in an increasingly global society? How is it subjected to meaningful analysis? Does it enjoy or qualify for specialized accreditation? Has the program successfully shifted the delivery of the curriculum to meet the changing needs of its clientele (for example, intensive courses and evening and weekend formats)?

Adaptability to Technology. What is the degree to which this program has taken advantage of advancements in technology to enhance learning, reinforce computer skills and computer literacy to prepare students for the higher-tech world in which they will live and work, attract technological support to the institution, enhance research, and enhance program-related public service?

Equipment, Facilities, and Other Resources. Programs differ widely in the physical resources required to deliver them. Mark Hopkins required only a log to support the teacher at one end and the student at the other. A program in biomedical engineering, on the other hand, is more complicated. This measure purports to evaluate the program on its capital capacities. How current are equipment and materials? What is the degree of modernization of laboratories and specialized facilities necessary to ensure that students are adequately prepared? How significant are the program holdings in the library and other learning centers? What is the degree of student and faculty access to electronic sources of program information? To what extent are the facilities conducive to quality learning experiences?

All of these measures of inputs represent this dimension of quality. They are the items typically counted in traditional accreditation reviews, departmental self-studies, and institutional profiles. One added dimension should be reviewed and answered as a part of the program prioritization process: What resources will it take to bring this program up to a high level of quality?

Criterion 5: Quality of Program Outcomes

Over the past thirty years, focus in higher education has shifted away from inputs and toward outcomes. Spurred by more sophisticated analysis techniques to measure impact and reinforced by regional accrediting bodies, notably the Southern Association of Colleges and Schools, an outcomes approach places the emphasis on assessing performance (Banta and others, 1993; Banta, Lund, Black, and Oblander, 1996). What examples of exemplary performance does the program demonstrate? In the area of student outcomes, what are test scores on nationally standardized instruments that measure attainment? How have the graduates fared on the GRE, the LSAT, the MCAT, and others? What congruence exists between intended and actual learning outcomes? What are the degrees of student satisfaction, alumni satisfaction, employer satisfaction? In the case of performance programs—music, drama, art—what evidence is there of client outcomes? Do alumni records and placement data give insights into program success? What is the track record of the graduates on state professional licensure and certification examinations? For two-year programs, did students articulate well into upper-division success at the receiving institutions? How successful are program graduates in seeking graduate and professional admission? Our programs are designed for intellectual and social development; did they succeed? In sum, what is the demonstrable effectiveness of the program in preparing students for the future?

Faculty outcomes measure the productivity of this critical resource. How well do program faculty achieve in measures of teaching effectiveness? (One institution, for its own reasons, measured the extent to which perceived grade inflation had taken place, by program, and accordingly counted negative points in the quality teaching outcomes criterion.) What is the track record of the program faculty in producing research accepted in juried publications or peer-reviewed electronic scholarship? What recognition do faculty bring the program in the area of public service? What results can be documented for program quality? Is there external validation of quality? The program has no doubt added value to the clientele it serves. What evidence is there of this important dimension? What is the degree to which the outcomes mirror best practices of similar institutions? Finally, how has the program brought beneficial recognition to the institution?

Assessing quality outcomes is generally regarded as more difficult and less precise than assessing quality inputs. As accreditation standards shift toward outcomes, however, more experience is gained and shared among institutions. Stronger institutions are secure enough to invite external peer review for some of this analysis, similar to the practice of using content specialists outside the institution to help judge worthiness for faculty tenure decisions. As with most other criteria, some programs will be better able than others to demonstrate measurable outcomes because, concerned about their impact, they have been collecting relevant information for years.

Criterion 6: Size, Scope, and Productivity of the Program

Easily quantifiable, this criterion looks at hard numbers. How many students (clients, customers, patrons, as appropriate) are being served? How many faculty and staff are assigned? What other resources are committed? What are the number of credit hours generated? Degrees or certificates awarded? Services rendered? Research developed? Creative efforts produced? Attendance at performances? How productive is the program?

What is the scope of the program—its breadth and depth? Is the academic content of the discipline honestly represented with respect to breadth and depth? On smaller campuses, individual faculty members are given the unenviable—and some would say impossible—task of covering an entire discipline. With the growth of knowledge, this is becoming increasingly untenable. At larger institutions, however, a discipline may have become skewed, due to faculty interests, and may not be providing adequate content exposure to its students. The English department, for example, may be overloaded with eighteenth-century English literature specialists when exposition is the primary requirement for most of its service obligations to the rest of the campus. Political science may be neglecting public law and administration by overemphasizing international area studies. Taken as a whole, is there sufficient critical mass? Is the program of sufficient size and scope to affirm that it can be conducted effectively?

In some cases, I have seen one or two people try to constitute an entire department, valiantly attempting to offer majors and multiple specialties and stretched too thin to do so effectively. Students become seriously shortchanged as a result, and quality suffers. Would it not be better to reduce this presence to a few service courses or eliminate it altogether, reallocating those resources to programs of higher priority? Analysis in this area may raise ancillary but critical policy questions: What is the minimum number of faculty, staff, and students required to be designated as a department? Does information analysis suggest opportunities for consolidation or restructuring?

Criterion 7: Revenue and Other Resources Generated by the Program

Typically programs and departments are seen as cost centers, not revenue producers. In fact, programs may be said to generate resources in addition to depleting them, and it is important to understand the net balance between the two. Revenue may be program driven or program specific, and this analysis is required for the institution to appreciate fully the impact a program may have on its overall fiscal affairs. Resources may be generated from a number of areas:

- Enrollments. What internal subsidy would be appropriate to account for the enrollment the program attracts?

- Cross-subsidies. What subsidy should the program receive for services it provides other internal programs? Is the program a net payer or a net receiver?

- Research grants. From its research grant activity, what has the program generated for itself, and what does it receive as a result of overhead or indirect cost recovery for the institution? How reliant is the institution on this source of funds for purposes other than the direct program costs?

- Fundraising. Is the institution a recipient of development or advancement dollars or other gifts because of the program? How significant are program-restricted funds, and should this be a factor in judging the relative worth of this program?

- Equipment grants. Has the program attracted equipment or other capital items to the institution, and what is the use of these items by other programs? Do these items represent outlays the institution would have had to make without them, and at what value?

- Other sources. Does the program generate revenues from admission fees, special fees, laboratory fees, ticket revenues, other user fees, or by other means that help offset some or all of the expenses associated with the program?

- Potential revenue. Are there conditions of anticipated gifts, bequests, or endowment that require maintaining the program? I have seen two contrary examples of this factor at work. In the first, a university retained a program it was considering dropping when it became known that a local benefactor had died, leaving the program $1 million. In the second, a private college had been retaining a program it thought unwise to cut only because of perceived alumni allegiance. The allegiance turned out to be mythical. When alumni were advised that the program would be eliminated unless sufficient dollars were forthcoming to save it, there was scant response. The program was eliminated, saving the college hundreds of thousands of dollars and freeing up facilities and space for higher-priority purposes.

Resources, of course, mean more than money. A major resource of a program can be its relationships. What is the degree to which the program has cultivated relationships that benefit the institution? Examples include the following:

- Community colleges or technical schools and program-specific training relationships
- University-corporate relationships that lead to graduate enrollments, consulting arrangements, research contracts, and corporate philanthropy
- Economic development relationships with communities that are job creating and otherwise mutually beneficial
- Joint ventures or projects between the program and other entities that are beneficial to the campus.

Active, dynamic programs look for ways to reach out to the larger world in order to secure feedback about their curriculum relevance and to generate additional support. Moribund programs do not. What value should be placed on this outreach dimension?

Criterion 8: Costs and Other Expenses Associated with the Program

This criterion seeks to measure all relevant costs, direct and indirect, that are associated with delivering the program. Cost accounting systems in higher education have become increasingly sophisticated. Whether the institution is accounting for its costs in an advanced way or not, the goal should be to assign the total costs of the institution to the sum of its programs. Analyzing program costs, as against program revenues, is a key criterion. Obviously some programs are more expensive than others. Some are more productive. Decisions made solely on this criterion would result in a seriously imbalanced institution at the same time that certain programs may be found to be too costly for the resources available.

Two additional cost-related questions should be answered for each program. One concerns efficiencies. What demonstrable efficiencies in the way the program is operated (or which could be inaugurated) are beneficial to the institution? Programs that have been better than others at driving efficiencies or improving productivity should be given appropriate credit.

The other concerns investments. What investment in new resources will be required to bring the program up to a high level of quality? This question, also asked in Criterion 4, is repeated here because of its importance to effective planning. If it is true that most programs in the United States are underfunded, it is also true that resources will be grossly insufficient to bring them all to a level of distinction worthy of their institutions' achievable aspirations. When honest answers to this question are received and analyzed, they will reveal the true depth and breadth of the resources imbalance problem. In many cases the issue will hit home for the first time: We simply cannot afford to be what we have become. The resources—faculty, staff, equipment, space—required to deliver the program the way the institution, its mission, and its stakeholders expect will run more than are reasonably available. And the serious decisions about what to keep and what to enhance can finally be made with realistic information.

There are success stories attendant to this matter. At a private university, for example, the business program was ultimately judged to be in high demand but of low quality. An estimate of $5 million was required to bring the program up to the accreditation standards of the American Assembly of Collegiate Schools of Business (AACSB). Rather than cut the program or permit it to continue to languish, the president decided to mount a special fundraising campaign to meet the higher-quality expectations of AACSB accreditation. In other instances, by contrast, the needs of the program were seen to be insurmountable. Because the resources required would never be forthcoming, the program was mercifully terminated. Through this analysis, institutions can rediscover the axiom that quality costs.

Criterion 9: Impact, Justification, and Overall Essentiality of the Program

In many ways, this criterion is the summative measure of why the program deserves to be continued or strengthened at the institution. Many colleges refer to this as the catch-all criterion—the category where anything else of relevance about the program, not previously inventoried, fits. Several questions are raised: What impact has this program had or does it promise to have? What are the benefits to the institution of offering this program? What is the connecting relationship between this program and achievement of the institution's mission? How essential is this program to the institution? What is the relationship of this program to the success of other programs?

Practical examples of the use of this criterion generally involve programs that are buttressed or considered essential because of their academic centrality. It is hard to imagine a college without a strong presence in English or mathematics, for example. The programs may need shoring up, but they are considered essential. A good philosophy department chair once graphically depicted for me his vision that philosophy is the central discipline, with all others emanating from it. A dedicated member of almost any other academic discipline holds similar guild-centric views. But however an institution defines what is central, some programs perforce become marginal.

Certain disciplines have apparently been thus typified on campus after campus. Declines across the country are seen in the offering of foreign languages, for example, and in programs in anthropology and geography. The presence of physical sciences on many campuses may now exclude geology as a specialty. Recently minted programs in ethnic or gender studies or interdisciplinary programs that seek to integrate studies in area or geographic or thematic ways are often victims of too tight a definition of essentiality. In general, the smaller the institution is, the tighter the academic focus needs to be. And yet the program closure decisions made by some institutions can create opportunities for others. If a discipline is being phased out at one college, it might be strengthened at another. Answers to the essentiality questions are thus intertwined with the institution's strategic planning. Gauging a program's worth here is also appropriate in terms of its responsiveness to the unique characteristics of the sheltering institution. Does this program serve people in ways that no other program does? Does it respond to a unique societal need that the institution values? To what extent does this program help the institution differentiate itself from the crowd of other colleges and universities? In the final analysis, how is this program linked with the institution's overall strategy?

Criterion 10: Opportunity Analysis of the Program

This final criterion seeks to enfranchise the providers of the program in suggesting how the program might seize opportunities heretofore not considered by the institution. Subsequent decision makers should take advantage of the best ideas that surface in this analysis. As Criterion 1 looked to the past to assess the program, Criterion 10 looks to the future. The program prioritization process will impose stress on decision makers to decide about program reduction, elimination, consolidation, or even enrichment. It has been my experience that because program providers are closest to the action, more or less aware of relative possibilities, and faced with the reality that some kind of change will likely occur, they emerge at this point with truly innovative suggestions. The inclusion of this criterion encourages those suggestions.

Among the questions are these: What external environmental factors affect the institution in such ways that opportunities are created? Which among these might this program seize? Are there opportunities for the program to continue, but in a different format? Are there opportunities for productivity gains that, if followed, would salvage the program? Can we implement cost-containment measures due to restructuring or technological innovation? Does the program have an information technology strategic plan (see Fink, 1997; Graves, Henshaw, Oberlin, and Parker, 1997)? What about cooperative or collaborative relationships with other programs? With other institutions? What exciting, creative ways can program faculty and staff put their best case forward by advancing new ideas about the program? What are the opportunities for combining courses or sections or other program units? Where is duplication avoidable? What is the potential for reengineering the way the curriculum is delivered? What is the relationship of the program to emerging trends in distance learning? To asynchronous learning? Is this program poised to transform itself in new and different ways?

Examples of adaptations made by colleges and universities abound. Universities, needing remediation courses for incoming freshmen, contract with local community colleges to offer them. Former "departments," no one of which has the resources to merit that designation, merge with similar specialties to form a new administrative unit. Formerly decentralized sections of technical writing merge. The history program at University X loses its French historian and shares with nearby University Y its intellectual historian in exchange. Interinstitutional collaboration to justify cost offers students instruction in foreign languages (you cover Russian; we will cover Mandarin). Some specialties formerly delivered traditionally are offered electronically. Program emphasis is shifted from on-campus status to adult, continuing, or distance education. Program costs are off-loaded to alternate funds. Scarce resources are shared among several programs. And interdepartmental collaboration is rewarded, not punished.

This opportunity analysis yields essential ideas of value to the institution's future. It seeks to enable faculty and staff to actualize a fundamental reality: what was done in the past was appropriate for the past, but the world is different today, and we must commit ourselves to preparing our graduates for their future. Not all program providers will respond; some will cling tenaciously to the status quo. Many program providers, however, will accept the challenge of this criterion and become a part of reshaping their programs for the future.

Chapter Six

Measuring, Analyzing, Prioritizing

> Everything that exists, exists in some amount and
> can be measured to some degree.

Within the community of business management consultants, the legendary approach of the Boston Consulting Group to measuring, analyzing, and prioritizing a company's business products is often cited. A business product was measured, according to this approach, by assessing two criteria, market growth and market share. From this analysis, products were judged to be one of four types: stars, providing high market growth and high market share; cash cows, offering low growth but high share; question marks, exhibiting high growth but low share; and dogs, representing low growth and low share. For a company to be successful, stars were to be built, cash cows maintained, question marks built or dropped, and dogs eliminated. This system no doubt worked for hundreds of businesses: clarity was attained, focus was achieved, and everybody in the organization understood the priorities.

Higher education does not have it as easy. Although there are no doubt stars and dogs among a college's products—its programs—the criteria required to measure a program's efficacy are more complex and the bottom line fuzzier. To the extent that the reallocation of resources requires program prioritization, campuses will need to follow a process that accommodates its unique needs and culture as it undertakes this important analysis. What is offered in this chapter are recommendations on how to proceed, based on experiences observed in multiple campus settings.

Preparation

The overall effort will require serious consideration of basic issues. Once the critical elements are in place, the campus is adequately prepared to undertake program prioritization.

Understanding the Need for Reform. To what extent is the campus aware of the resources problem, the need to address over-programming, and the likelihood that new resources will mostly come from reallocation of existing resources? Charles Neff observed over a quarter-century ago that "planning is more than a technique; it is technique plus vision and commitment" (Neff, 1971, p. 116). And part of securing commitment is building awareness of the overall vision for the organization. The noble goals of any vision cannot be attained without the people, money, and other resources committed in more focused ways. Understanding the need for reform is therefore required for commitment to reform.

Identifying Responsible Leadership. How committed and visible are the president and executive team members? What is the state of trustee readiness? Has appropriate leadership been empowered throughout the institution to champion the coming process? Has the case been made in a compelling way sufficient to achieve the task ahead? Will the needs of the institution transcend its personalities?

Reaffirming Institutional Mission. Since the mission of the institution is the grid against which all subsequent program decisions are to be made, serious questions must be answered: Is the campus of high consensus about its role and scope? Is there a common sense of whom it serves and what it does? Do stakeholders recognize that it can no longer afford to be what it has become?

Defining What Constitutes a Program. Is the process to follow disciplined by a common definition of "program"? Have all resources of the institution been arrayed into discrete program components? Is the distinction between a program and the administrative entity that shelters it made clear?

Selecting Appropriate Criteria. Are sufficient data likely to be available to support all ten criteria? Will the criteria selected, once sustained by information, yield the results expected from this process? Since these decisions may be challenged in numerous ways—and possibly in the courts—has careful thought been given to the academically sound reasons for choosing criteria and assigning weights to them? Only after these critical elements are in place is the campus adequately prepared to undertake program prioritization.

Process Design and Management

The campus should clarify both the design of the program prioritization process and who will manage it. Questions will abound, and rumors will circulate. Participants need to know where to get straight answers, and they will need to feel that answers are consistently given. The institution should publish a timetable for the process, which balances the urgency of the task with the reasonableness of the time constraints of its participants.

It has been my uniform experience on all campuses that the office of academic affairs serves as the manager of the data collection and analysis phases of the process. The reasons for this arrangement are clear enough. Such offices routinely request, collect, and analyze data about academic programs for a variety of reasons—planning, budgeting, accreditation—and for issuance of myriad reports. The institutional research office supports this function with its relevant databases and expertise. Overall management of the process, however, is usually the responsibility of the president, because the eventual decisions will likely require approval from both the president and the board of trustees. While it is important for the relationship between the president and the provost to be nearly symbiotic in most cases in higher education administration, it is essential throughout the prioritization and reallocation processes. As often happens in stressful times, campus participants who feel threatened may try to foment a breach between the two key officers of the institution. Neither the president nor the provost can permit this to happen. The best presidents and provosts agree to disagree behind closed doors and to present unity to the campus they have the responsibility to lead.

An example of a process agenda, adopted by a public land grant university, is contained in Resource B.

Data Collection

Data will become more useful if they are collected in common formats. Some of these items will no doubt be readily available because of past institutional practice: cost per credit hour generated; student major demand data from the Astin (1998) study or from ACT and SAT reports; information collected by the admissions office on demand trend lines and new student profiles; marketing studies of competitive institutions; comparative information on results from the Student Satisfaction Inventory; data maintained for specialized accreditation purposes; faculty workload data; information advanced to supplement tenure and promotion requests; evaluations of teaching effectiveness; grade distribution patterns; past budget requests to help assess the extent of program needs; and the list goes on. Other data will have to come from the programs themselves: results of alumni satisfaction surveys; feedback reports from employers; acceptance records of graduates into graduate or professional programs; anecdotal information about program history, development, and successes; analysis of program content breadth and depth; utilization of and access to computing facilities and services; maintenance of academic advising loads; and past efforts at improving productivity.

For several years now, an "assessment movement" has swept the academy, spearheaded by the American Association for Higher Education (AAHE) and buttressed by several regional accrediting bodies, governing boards, and legislatures. Numerous conferences, publications, and suggestions have emanated from AAHE on the need for campuses to communicate—through better measurement—the value of their learning programs. These efforts have had varying impact on campuses across the country (Banta, Lund, Black, and Oblander, 1996; Donald, 1997). A relatively new force in the profession, the Society of College and University Planning, has assembled institutional research and college planning professionals who have stressed better data collection, shared information across campuses for comparative purposes, and authored publications aimed at more sophisticated means of measurement in postsecondary education. For years the American Association of Collegiate Registrars and Admissions Officers (AACRAO) has published common guides and useful templates as standards for effective records management. Both AACRAO published reports and its new electronic data interchange advancements can prove helpful. Public colleges and universities have recently developed a series of reports to enhance comparable information reporting. These standardized reporting conventions may be applicable to independent institutions as well (Mortimer, 1995–1997). The regional accrediting agencies have now uniformly shifted emphasis toward outcomes measures and evidence of change based on outcomes.

Campuses are scampering to present program data in new ways in order to secure favorable external reviews. At some institutions, however, it appears that shelters have been built to provide isolation from the information explosion. Such information as exists is scattered, irrelevant, or unfathomable. In a few instances, it does not even exist. There is no institutional research presence. For these places, construction is required and may necessitate a basic recapturing process to secure information necessary for the prioritization. Information abounds, however, on other campuses, notably public institutions under increased scrutiny from coordinating boards and legislative oversight committees demanding greater accountability.

What is required in all cases is a format that realistically accomplishes its purpose: to enable consistent and comparative analysis among all programs. Some program purveyors will object to the inclusion of certain formats. The correlation between their objection and perceived low performance on the particular criterion is sometimes noteworthy. But one essential element of data collection is participation. By including all stakeholders in the process of collecting and advancing data, particularly data that have not heretofore been sought, campus participants become more engaged. Interest and motivation to participate increase, and presumably better decisions can result.

The Rating System

Once data are collected, analysis begins by rating the information according to categories previously announced. Following are examples of how campuses have typically undertaken comparative analysis. But an institution should not feel constrained by these approaches. Indeed, new and often creative ways to engage in measurement often emerge, and as long as the college uniformly applies its novel approach across all programs, I encourage the initiative.

For quality input measures, campuses have used multiple-point rating systems, typically three ("High," "Medium," "Low"), four ("Exceptional," "Strong," "Adequate," "Weak"), five, or seven, the last using a Likert-type scale for measuring intensity. Variations include "Excellent," "Adequate," and "Insufficient." Trend lines might be assessed "Growing," "Stable," or "Declining." Quality outcomes, more subjectively assessed, typically follow a seven-point scale to measure importance ("Not important at all," "Not very important," "Somewhat unimportant," "Neutral," "Somewhat important," "Important," and "Very important") or level of agreement ("Strongly disagree," "Agree," "Somewhat agree," "Neutral," "Somewhat disagree," "Disagree," and "Strongly disagree") or satisfaction (with similar gradations). Obviously some criteria are more readily quantifiable than others—for example, indirect costs allocated, revenues generated, number of holdings, grade point averages and test scores, square feet assigned, percentage of graduates passing state licensure on the first try, student retention, or percentage of occupancy. Still other criteria can be rated according to extent of sufficiency ("Does not meet expectations" "Meets expectations," and "Exceeds expectations").

Some campuses use the traditional five-point grading scale and assess criteria by awarding "A" through "F," denoting excellence through failure. Others approach certain criteria with simple "Yes-No" or "Essential-Not essential" scores. All such measures should be proximate to the criterion being used, understandable to participants, and capable of being comparatively assessed.

Some campuses engage outside consultants or peer reviewers to rate programs independently. One university campus had an interim dean heading a key college and, to try to ensure that the college's programs were objectively rated, retained a national expert in the professional field to rate the programs independently, in addition to the on-campus rating scheduled for all programs. Other campuses call on outside help to rate programs, using different rating systems as a check on reliability, or the same systems, as an additional check on validity. In one such instance involving a private university, the consultant evaluated program clusters with the 100-point system shown in Exhibit 6.1. This approach yielded a matrix with program clusters aligned along one axis and the criteria with assigned points along the other. The matrix permitted campus officials to see at a glance an overview of relative program strengths and weaknesses; observe overall point scores in relation to all programs; begin to target certain program areas more carefully to understand the specific reasoning behind a particular rating; and pinpoint possible areas for enhancement, consolidation, or reduction.

The use of outside consultants should be seen as a supplement to and not a replacement for on-campus participation and involvement. There is no substitute for the engaged participation and expanded understanding resulting from objective, campuswide participation.

The state of Tennessee has led the way for nearly twenty years in converting performance measurement to performance funding.

Exhibit 6.1. Quantifying Program Criteria (A Private University Example).

A. National Demand (10 points)

Extent to which the program is identified in national incoming student demand data. Total program preferences break roughly into quintiles:

2.0 percent or greater	10 points
1.0–1.9 percent	8 points
0.7–0.9 percent	6 points
0.3–0.6 percent	4 points
0.0–0.2 percent	2 points

B. Local Demand Trend (10 points)

Trend line, past five years, fall to fall, by program. Trend identified as increasing, steady, or declining.

Increasing	10 points
Steady	5 points
Declining	0 points

C. Quality (15 points)

Judgment about program quality, based on information supplied in program portfolios.

Quality inputs: Faculty credentials, student inputs above norm, other input information   1 to 5 points

Quality outcomes: Outcomes data, placement reports, graduate information/feedback, employer information, publications and creative works, other outcomes information
1 to 5 points

External validation: Specialized accreditation, external awards, other validation of quality   1 to 5 points

D. Size (15 points)

Relative size of program, as measured by student credit hours generated, spring term, in rank order, by quintiles.

Rank: Upper 20 percent	15 points
Next 20 percent	12 points
Next 20 percent	9 points
Next 20 percent	6 points
Bottom 20 percent	3 points

E. Productivity (15 points)

Student credit hours generated, divided by faculty resources, in rank order, by quintiles.

Rank: Upper 20 percent	15 points
Next 20 percent	12 points
Next 20 percent	9 points
Next 20 percent	6 points
Bottom 20 percent	3 points

F. Internal Impact (15 points)

Degree to which program serves other departments or generates for other departments.

Voluntary impact	5 points
Required impact	5 points
Required impact, multiple programs	5 points

G. Other Justification (20 points)

Validity of justification claims; degree of essentiality to mission of university; other benefits of sustaining the program.

Touted as a stimulus for campus improvement as well as an accountability mechanism, Tennessee's performance funding standards for its public institutions have been emulated to varying degrees in several states. The standards in place for 1993 through 1997 are instructive:

1. Accreditation

2. Major field tests

3. Measurement of general education outcomes

4. Alumni and enrolled-student surveys

5. Improvement actions taken to remedy identified weaknesses

6. Peer review of nonaccreditable undergraduate programs

7. Master's program reviews (universities) or placement (two-year institutions)

8. Enrollment goals for campus-specific groups

9. Persistence to graduation for minority and all students

10. Mission-specific objectives

Each has an associated weight of 10 points, for a total possible score of 100.

Although these are performance standards for institutions, and public ones at that, the model may have applicability for programs within institutions, since programs contribute to the achievement of overall institutional expectations. These standards are presented here as another example of academic weights and measures at work (Bogue and Brown, 1982; Banta and others, 1996).

Levels of Judgment

Judgments about program prioritization must be informed and supported by the data. The philosophic underpinning for this approach has its roots in goal-based, criterion-referenced evaluation, as opposed to a political-negotiative model, which emphasizes the political, not technical, nature of measurement and seeks to negotiate results among the competing demands of various stakeholders. This approach may have some legitimacy for certain stakeholders (particularly for those with current influence), but its explicitly political nature detracts from the credibility of a more technical approach. I cannot emphasize too strongly that politics as usual on the campus will bear no resemblance to the standards of accountability expected by external publics—parents, donors, policymakers, the general public—who support higher education.

Judgments about programs should be made in ascending order of institutional responsibility. That is, rankings of programs, based on the data, should be made first by department or division heads and then on three ascending levels: first by directors or deans, then by vice presidents, and finally by the president, whose recommendations go to the board of trustees for final approval. The levels and titles vary, of course, by campus. In smaller institutions, directors typically rank programs and then send recommendations to the provost and president, who act as a unified level of review prior to board action.

Judgments require extraordinary care and analysis. The analysis at each level should bring to bear on the task the cumulative experience of the judge. Key questions about the institution's mission and its future, about how clients are to be served and their needs met, and about costs required to bring the programs up to a high level of quality are all important. By avoiding these questions, institutional leaders run the risk of settling for mediocrity, admitting that egalitarianism is the prevailing value, deferring the tough realities of the very near future, surrendering their stewardship of the institution to the status quo, and basing the future on unrealistically winning some phantom academic lottery.

It is important to fix responsibility at each level of judgment. At each higher level, a more institution-wide perspective will be required. For example, an institution-wide decision may be to retain all programs in division A and two-thirds of the programs in division B, while eliminating all programs in division C. Each higher level of decision making obtains the benefit of the cumulative wisdom of each lower level, but adds its broader perspective to judgments made in the best interest of the entire institution.

Many campuses, particularly those with a desire to present as open a process as possible, schedule hearings at each level. A dean may publish her or his tentative rankings of programs, and then conduct a hearing to explain the reasoning behind the rankings and to receive suggestions and feedback before finalizing the decisions and passing them on to the next level. I have seen this process yield information that proved invaluable to the process, and in every instance, subsequent decisions were better made because they were better informed. It also gives the lie to the myth that often surfaces that "these decisions have already been cast in stone." Involvement by interested parties also serves to facilitate creativity and build trust. A similar hearing process would ensue at the vice presidential level, and so on.

All participants operate from the same mission statement, the same program criteria, and the same weights. Yet decisions perforce will vary from level to level, depending on the relative perspective and understanding that the judge possesses about the institution's total needs and opportunities. To the extent possible, this judgment should be shared with the campus community. In this way, the process can assist stakeholders to expand their frames of reference, appreciate a more holistic perspective, and understand deeper levels of the interdependencies the campus represents.

Ranking by Categories

I have yet to see a campus rank-order all its programs, although I suppose that is possible to do. Given the large number of programs typically found on a campus and the inability to make ranking decisions with penultimate precision, categories of rankings are typically more useful. The most common approaches are to rank programs by thirds (top—to be considered for enrichment; middle—to be retained at present level of support; and lower—to be reduced, phased out, or consolidated) or by quintiles:

Upper 20 percent: Candidates for enrichment

Next 20 percent: Retained at higher level of support

Next 20 percent: Retained at neutral level of support

Next 20 percent: Retained at lower level of support

Lowest 20 percent: Candidates for reduction, phasing out, consolidation

There is no room for grade inflation. To be effective—and to yield resources for important reallocation purposes—*each category must house an equal number of programs*. Stated another way, in a quintile approach, 20 percent of the programs are placed in the first category, 20 percent in the second, until the end. The key here is to prioritize, to make available for resource reallocation decisions an honest determination that all programs are not equal, and that some share greater congruency than others with the future of the institution.

Decisions

Decisions—about program enrichment, consolidation, reduction, or elimination—are recommended by the president after undergoing the prioritization process, but can be made only by the governing board. Only the board should have the authority to close programs, and this authority should not be delegated (*The Board's Role in Accreditation*, 1982).

The board will want to satisfy itself about the validity of the entire process and will need to consider numerous factors: faculty employment interests, the academic needs of students currently enrolled in affected programs, the interdependent impact a closing might have on other programs, the likely reactions of various constituencies, and other factors influencing the board's responsibilities as the ultimate steward of the institution.

Chapter Seven

Anticipating Process Issues

People tend to support that which they help
to create.

It is unlikely that all issues and concerns surrounding the prioritization of programs can be completely anticipated; nevertheless, it is possible to benefit from the experiences of other campuses. Here are the most common issues that surface.

"Shouldn't the administration have to prioritize its programs as well?"

Most of the cost cutting has taken place historically in the administrative, nonacademic cost centers of the campus. The NACUBO benchmarking and business process reengineering activities are almost exclusively about nonacademic processes, for example. At the same time, faculty who are about to undergo a rigorous reform process want to make sure no other resource allocation rival misses out on the experience. Administrative officers, by contrast, will use the argument that they "already gave" when donations were sought for the cause. This argument is usually not convincing, however true it might be. The specter of a process to right the listing institutional ship, with only half the people on board doing their share to help, is not politically acceptable at most campuses. If we are truly a community, the argument goes, then we need to undergo this analysis as a community.

Campuses tend to handle this issue in one of three ways. First, where the institution can demonstrate that administration cost cutting in the recent past was of such magnitude that academic programs were indeed spared at the expense of programs in administration, business affairs, or student life, such nonacademic programs are exempted from the process.

A second approach is to apply the same process and the same criteria against all programs, academic and nonacademic alike. This has worked successfully, although some institutions find the criteria, written primarily for academic programs, to be somewhat stifling or inconsistent when applied to administrative programs.

Finally, some campuses have asked me to write criteria that would apply specifically to nonacademic programs, so that the prioritization process could be undertaken in a "separate but equal" format. An example of such a separate review, which I believe is applicable to most campuses, is contained in Resource C. It contains thirteen items for securing information from each administrative program and suggests nine questions for analyzing the results.

"Let us keep this program. It doesn't really take any resources."

Sooner or later in the process, both academic and nonacademic departments will discover a program that they know cannot pass muster when analyzed fairly against the criteria, but they attempt to retain it on the grounds that it "does not expend institutional resources." A typical example is a department that operates a fairly sound baccalaureate program but tries to offer a master's degree (in which few if any students are actually enrolled) "on the side." This practice represents an academic stretch. The argument goes something like this: "We already have the faculty, buildings, and equipment in place [for the baccalaureate program]. Why not let us keep our M.A. program?" An intensive review of the graduate program in question, however, usually reveals minimal enrollments, heavy cross-listing with undergraduate courses or with courses offered by ancillary departments, library holdings insufficient to the deeper level required for graduate study, inadequate time and attention paid to the specialized research and advising needs of the graduate students, and other indicators of shoddy quality. The issue surfaces because the department may think it is benefiting from some vaunted graduate program status. The reality is that the student would be better off enrolling in a solid graduate program elsewhere, and the department would be better off focusing its limited time, money, and attention on what it does best.

A nonacademic example is usually found in the athletic department. Additional so-called minor sports are offered with the claim that no real drain on resources occurs. Not so. Or a student services program may overextend itself, proffering services that students soon figure out are beyond the scope of the staff's professional competencies.

All programs require resources. They tap from the time, treasure, and talent pool available to the institution. Stated another way, if a program truly consumes no resources, it is not a program. Falling for the "it takes no resources" argument further diminishes institutional focus.

"This process can't be done on top of everything else we have to do."

A common lament of faculty is the lack of time to accomplish everything. Indeed, there are some faculty members who are so committed to their teaching, research, advising, service, and campus responsibilities that it is not uncommon to measure 80- to 100-hour work-weeks for them. It is also possible to get run over in the parking lot on any given day at 1:30 P.M. by other faculty, rushing to escape the campus. It is a fortunate college that enjoys a preponderance of the former and a minimum of the latter.

It is also fair to note that faculty are trained to explore matters in depth and with the standard of care that requires large concentrations of time. Good thinkers require adequate time to reflect critically. While some would criticize faculty generally as incapable of making decisions, I find that oversimplistic. It is more likely that the academically trained mind, geared toward the pursuit of truth, is usually unwilling to rest, even on some tentative version of the truth. There is always more to learn, to analyze, to test. Bringing things to conclusion (which administrators have to do on a daily basis) is seen as hopelessly and needlessly premature. That is why every scholarly research report ends with the admonition, "... further study is needed." How to balance the pursuit of the best possible decisions with the best available information, within the pressures of planning, budget, and catalogue deadlines, is indeed a challenge.

In response to this issue, I believe that academic program prioritization must be seen as an *extraordinary process requiring a suspension of ordinary behaviors*. The institution's future is at stake. If meaningful faculty involvement is desired, then accommodation of the time to participate fully should be made. Could the plethora of campus committees and the inordinate number of committee meetings be suspended for a period of time, and that time better devoted to prioritization? Could some parts of the prioritization take place primarily in the fall (springtime on campus is not a season usually conducive to judicious decisions) or between terms? Could release time be reallocated from current purposes to this purpose? Most campuses are fully capable of undertaking a rigorous prioritization process within an academic year. Some under real pressure have done it in three months. In other instances, prioritization was seen as part of a longer, multiple-year strategic planning process. And in still other cases, most of the data could be collected centrally, thus reducing a portion of the burden on the program-offering departments.

In any event, the issue truly is about *prioritization:* what is the relative value of this process, over and against campus routines, in attempting to secure the benefits of participation for the success of the institution? The collegiate community's positive answer to this question can lay the necessary foundation for success.

"We've done this kind of thing before, but nobody paid attention. There were no results."

A common criticism of program review is that the results are not linked to planning or budgeting. With program prioritization, however, linkage is inseparable. The institution's leaders must commit to decide on the recommendations and to act on the results. Indeed, the entire process should not be undertaken absent a concomitant resolve to produce results that will tighten the focus and reallocate the resources of the institution. If this resolve is adequately communicated, participants will sense it. On more than one occasion, I have seen faculty come forward with extraordinarily good recommendations—about combining departments, reallocating faculty FTE by subject competency, and other matters that would not otherwise have dawned on the administration—but only when they were convinced that *this* time the institution meant business, and action was in fact going to take place.

"How deep do we have to cut?"

Many campuses initiate the prioritization process with a vague notion in mind that reallocation will take place, but they have not set a quantifiable target for either the cutting at one end or the enhancing at the other. Again, the answer to this question depends on the local situation and the campus-specific wisdom. Some campuses have announced target goals, stated in terms of dollars to be generated ("We will reallocate $1 million") or in percentages ("We shall reallocate 10 percent of resources from lower to higher priorities"). Proponents for this approach argue that it is necessary to know where—and when—to draw the line. By announcing goals in advance, it focuses the process and further gives incentive to strong programs that hope to benefit from additional resources to participate enthusiastically.

On the other hand, campuses have also discovered that the process yielded more (and in some cases, less) than targeted. Targets set in advance might prove unnecessarily arbitrary. Setting a hard and fast number to be achieved might create unnecessary frustration and limit the attainment of full potential.

"If you haven't heard a rumor by 10:00 A.M., start one."

Change is unsettling. Fear of change generates rumors, mis-communication, and distrust. While "enhanced communication" may be the most overworked recommendation applied to organizations of all kinds, it is patently accurate for colleges and universities engaged in prioritization. Campuses that have successfully mastered the communication challenge offer the following suggestions:

- Hold campuswide meetings to build awareness, update the participants as a whole, respond to questions, and reaffirm the goals of prioritization.
- Set up "rumor telephone hot lines" to correct misinformation as it unfolds.
- Bring in outside expert speakers to help build awareness, communicate context, and add credibility.
- Appoint cross-departmental task forces assigned the various "change" duties outlined in Chapter Three.
- Retain outside consultants or peer reviewers to ensure neutrality.
- Conduct periodic open hearings on program reports and specific recommendations to communicate openness to feedback.
- Publish a "Prioritization Newsletter" and create an on-line bulletin board to keep campus participants informed about each stage of the initiative.
- Provide constant reference to the goals, timetable, and expectations of the prioritization by campus and board leaders.
- Schedule regular interactive meetings between campus leadership and any oversight or steering committee appointed to oversee the process.

The price of open communication is that some information can be embarrassing or misleading. If, for example, a program is recommended for discontinuance at one level, word spreads to the program constituents, including students enrolled in the program, who react as though the decision were final. I have seen students withdraw from the institution, operating on the misassumption that the program was to be cut.

The alternative—to conduct the prioritization process in secret—is unacceptable. Meeting behind closed doors breeds suspicion. Resolution of this dilemma will require patience and understanding from all campus stakeholders—and a little help from the press.

The role of the campus and community press is itself an issue of some contention at many institutions. Presidents commiserate among themselves about their treatment at the hands of the press by sharing aphorisms: "The Constitution guarantees a free press, not a fair press." "Don't screw up on a slow news day." "Don't get in a spitting contest with people who buy ink by the barrel." "The press covers only crashes, not landings." "Editorial writers are those who rush down from the mountain after the battle is over and shoot the wounded."

Yet the writers of news stories about the campus and its change process can be invaluable adjuncts to an overall communication plan within prioritization. What is required is the ability to share context. One of the frustrating aspects of instruction for professors is that at the end of the term, just when the students finally understand the subject matter, they leave and are replaced by other students, and the professor must start all over again. It is the same with reporters. At most news organizations, education writers are typically at the bottom of the pecking order. They usually know little about higher education and may be anxious to move on to more glamorous beats. Turnover is high and interest is low. It is therefore critical for campus leaders to take the time to help build a sense of context for reporters. Share with them information about higher education trends and broader national events that affect the institution and how the campus stands on important characteristics relative to other institutions. Help reporters see motivating forces behind actions. Encourage writers to place events in an understandable context. The likelihood of that occurring is directly proportional to the early and consistent effort of college and university leaders to do a better job of building positive relationships with the media and telling their own stories (Footlick, 1997, 1998).

"What's to become of the affected students?"

As the process unfolds, it becomes clear that some programs will indeed have to be cut even though there are students enrolled in them. In addition to possible legal reasons for permitting students to complete programs to which the campus committed through publication of its catalogue, there are essential moral imperatives as well. It should be announced at the outset and communicated throughout the process and its implementation that students will not suffer as a result of program discontinuance. No institution should ignore this imperative. To fulfill this mandate will require careful planning, flexible scheduling, and one-on-one counseling with students, advisers, and program staff. In every instance I have seen it work splendidly.

"How does this process relate to our governance process?"

Governance in American higher education is a separate topic of profound import that has confounded outside observers about how things transpire in academe. One writer declared, "University governance is by and large a crazy quilt of hierarchies, committees, and overlapping jurisdictions, and almost anyone who is closely connected with it privately recognizes that it is archaic, inefficient, inhibitive to necessary change, and not even very comfortable any more" (Neff, 1971, p. 119).

But should the prioritization process, with its emphasis on mission-driven, data-enhanced, ascending levels of responsibility, be subject to the very governance system that, it can be argued, got the campus into program proliferation trouble in the first place? Each institution, with its own local sense of governance and operating within its special legal framework and unique culture, will have to accommodate the competing demands of this issue.

Those arguing to make use of the governance system as it stands will assert that all decisions regarding the curriculum must go through the requisite committees, councils, and senates ordained for those purposes. To do otherwise, it is argued, the results will not bear the same aegis of legitimacy as past curricular and program decisions. Some governance units are drawn strictly from and elected by constituency memberships (the faculty senate, the student government, the staff council), and they are accordingly proportionately representative of key stakeholders. By ignoring them, the results will be challenged as "undemocratic."

An opposing argument is that the governance units tend to base decisions on territorial and turf issues: Whose ox is being gored? Who wins or loses? Which fiefdoms can be breached? What cross-pressures need to be negotiated? Whose votes can be traded for what result? Besides being political, curriculum committees are essentially incremental: courses and programs are typically approved (or not) but rarely discontinued. Critics also point out that, contrary to widely accepted mythology, campuses are not democracies. In any event, most such governance committees do not feel they have the authority to discontinue courses and certainly not programs; only boards should have that authority. The mismatch between responsibility and authority is no more apparent than at the collision of this governance-participation issue. Most administrators would as soon disregard the normal governance process simply because the results will manifestly not fit the scope and depth of the task, or presumably rise to the high calling of this special purpose.

How should an institution tackle this one? Experiences on other campuses provide some options.

• One institution, for example, conducted the prioritization process, *then* sought the advice of the governance system before taking the results to the board of trustees for approval. In this instance, the governance units disagreed with the prioritization results; thus, conflicting recommendations went to the board. The board reasoned that all such governance units—and administrative officers, for that matter—were in fact recommendatory to the board and sided with the prioritization results.

• Another college board of trustees declared in advance that the prioritization process was an "extraordinary governance issue" requiring an extraordinary process. Several campuses have adopted this approach, some enfranchising those individuals likely to oppose or sabotage a prioritization and other campuses doing their best to exclude such individuals.

• A large private university mastered the problem by creating a special strategic planning committee with broad prioritization duties and created two "dotted-line" relationships to it, one from the operating units (schools and colleges) and the other from the governance committees and councils (called for this purpose "representative advisory units"). The effect was doubly beneficial: strategic planning and prioritization were seen as superordinate matters, and both academic units and governance units were empowered, albeit solely in subordinate, advisory capacities.

• Campuses with faculty unions must consult their contracts to determine the roles, if any, of bargaining units versus governance units or the opportunity to conduct prioritization through the processes suggested in this book. Although the complex issue of collective bargaining in higher education is not within the scope of this book, its meaning for prioritization is a knotty one: have faculty foreclosed their participation in this management-governance function by accepting membership in a bargaining unit?

The resolution of these thorny issues will no doubt presage the ability of the institution to redirect its future course. Such a resolution is probably overdue in all of American higher education.

Chapter Eight

Implementing Program Decisions

Ideas are not enough. It is only action that matters.
—*Peter Glen*

Once the analysis has been completed and the programs of the campus prioritized, important judgments are to be made that recommit the institution's resources in new ways so as to seize opportunities and sustain institutional integrity.

Decisions

Although each campus designs its own reallocation, experience indicates that resources typically are recommitted to enable five kinds of decisions.

Enrichment or Expansion of Existing Programs

Answers to the questions about resources required to bring programs up to a high level of quality (identified in Criteria 4 and 8) will yield a clearer and better picture of the true needs of programs at the institution. Balancing these needs against the likely resources available will reveal a gap that current and reasonably projected revenues cannot realistically be expected to bridge. At the same time, some programs emerge as the strengths of the campus, and they will deserve the support necessary to sustain and enhance their luster. This analysis may afford an opportunity to designate such programs as "centers [or peaks] of excellence." All great institutions build on their strengths; the value of highlighting real quality where it occurs reinforces excellence in those programs and becomes contagious. It spills over to other aspiring programs and creates a halo effect for the institution as a whole.

These programs may need additional faculty or staff support; equipment needs may be justified to bring program offerings more in line with current industry expectations; travel, sabbatical, or training dollars may be needed to ensure intellectual currency; space reallocation may be required. In numerous ways, rewarding stronger programs by reallocating from weaker programs sends the right message about institutional values and makes needed and often dramatic changes in the campus ethos.

Addition of New Programs

Analysis of demand, external or internal, may create awareness that the institution can benefit from the addition of new programs to its overall portfolio. Perhaps a new program idea, justified by solid analysis, has been on hold for some time, pending a resolution of the resources issue. Based on the same analysis, reducing or eliminating current programs that do not measure up will free the resources necessary to permit the institution to respond more meaningfully to its changing environment and the promise of a more mission-driven future. Cutting some programs while simultaneously adding others is not historically practiced in higher education, for all the reasons that have been identified. But this is a habit of successful organizations, and colleges and universities will need to acquire it.

Reduction of Programs

Analysis will reveal programs that are conducted with surplus resources—too many faculty assigned for the demand, too much space assigned for the program's real needs, equipment dollars unspent or spent unwisely, often due to historic incrementalism in budgeting or other irrational reasons. Perhaps attempting to offer a full-blown bachelor's degree cannot be justified by the demand or essentiality, and a minor in the subject matter will suffice. Such reductions in scope are usually accompanied by reductions in resources.

Consolidation or Restructuring of Programs

In every instance where program prioritization has been accomplished, resources are saved and reallocated to higher priorities by removing structural impediments. Each discipline does not need to operate with its own separate department if the numbers do not justify it. There may be overlap and needless duplication in course offering and curricular content. The larger the campus is, the more likely it is that multiple programs are offering essentially similar work in some cases. General or liberal studies programs may have grown to accommodate political interests of the providing departments and can be scaled back to a more cogent and academically coherent core. Students would certainly benefit from such a consolidation. Institutional requirements may be more historical than academically logical and can be rethought. Analysis often reveals that some courses have had no enrollees for the past few years. Why keep on the books such courses and the resources presumably poised to offer them?

Intense analysis during program prioritization can bring to the surface these and numerous other anomalies the institution can no longer afford to indulge. Possibly the administration of programs can stand consolidation. Perhaps the middle management layers have grown to accommodate needs or a time that no longer exists. Sharing of support and administrative resources is a small price to pay for greater efficiencies, for example.

Elimination of Programs

Many campuses try to get by on such scant support for programs that their providers realistically cannot continue to eke out an existence worthy of either the canons of the respective discipline or the goals of the institution. A merciful response is to cut the program. Institutions are loathe to take this step. Reasons include the fear that somehow outsiders will perceive the college to be less an academic enterprise than before. But an honest appraisal has to conclude that a program that is insufficiently supported—and relatively deficient in its effectiveness, efficiency, and essentiality—hardly strengthens the institution's reputation. Given the reaffirmed mission, the careful and forthright prioritization, the demonstrated needs of stronger programs, and the reality of scarce resources, the only honorable thing for the institution to do is to eliminate some of its lesser-ranked programs.

The board and the executive leadership will need to support the decisions made with the accompanying authority and resources to carry them out. It will take time and energy to implement program changes. Resource D contains excerpts from specific action plans undertaken by various colleges and universities after program prioritization decisions had been made. In the best cases, a strong linkage of decisions, planning, and budgeting mechanisms takes place.

Specific implementation strategies depend almost entirely on the legal, human resource, and policy characteristics unique to the institution. Advice on implementation therefore can only be general in nature. Specific campus applications are to be implemented only after thorough and informed consultation with legal advisers competent to assist the institution in fulfilling the ensuing process. Several logical steps, however, will help guide most campus implementation strategies.

Legal and Policy Implications

First among these implications is the assurance that appropriate institutional policies are in place and that those policies represent the best thinking about current law and higher education practice. Policies concerning program discontinuance, for example, should be in place and should reflect the procedural and substantive due process obligations of the institution. Across the country, institutions have adopted various policies governing financial, program, and institutional exigency. The definitions, threshold criteria, and procedures for triggering and implementing any or all of these categories should be carefully reviewed with competent legal counsel. Retrenched programs may lead to a reduction in force (RIF); if this is the case, extraordinary care must be taken in assessing the currency of the institution's policies to carry out a successful RIF. Program-specific reductions resulting from reallocation may require new or revised policies and procedures in these areas:

- Determination of the specific location of a faculty member's program area
- Determination of criteria for identifying specific faculty or staff to be reduced
- Adequacy of notice, effective dates of termination, or reduction of contractual rights and other procedures
- Provision for services, benefits, and employment opportunities
- Advisability of reassignment, reemployment, recall, or assistance possibilities
- Requirements for review or appeal

Affected faculty in programs to be discontinued may hold tenure. Tenure in higher education may be the most volatile issue confronting institutions today, particularly public institutions where intrusion by state officials is increasing. The historical purpose of tenure—to ensure an environment within which the concept of academic freedom is protected—has been somehow lost in the raging debate. In a growing number of state legislatures and on the agendas of numerous boards of trustees, the issue of tenure has devolved to a debate over job security versus institutional flexibility. The numbers are also reflective of the turmoil. At the same time that the percentage of full-time faculty holding tenure has remained constant (at 52 percent) between 1975 and 1995, the proportion of tenure-track full-time faculty has decreased from 29 to 20 percent. This decline has been accompanied by growth in the relatively new practice of employing full-time faculty on contracts rather than tenure track. In 1975 19 percent of full-time faculty worked on contracts; in 1995 the number had jumped to 28 percent (Wilson, 1998, p. A12). The reasons for these shifts are understandable. Governing boards, more focused on institutional fiscal realities, are recognizing that the granting of tenure constitutes a long-term commitment with a permanence not always warranted by enrollment shifts, curricular needs, and affirmative action imperatives. To the extent that boards see tenure decisions as unwisely constraining institutional flexibility, alternate arrangements, including multiple-year contracts, will continue to increase (Chait, Mortimer, Taylor, and Wood, 1985; Finnegan, 1997).

The meaning of tenure is particularly strained when decisions are necessarily made that cut specific academic programs. Historically tenure has been considered a contractually enforceable promise on the part of the institution to employ a faculty member for an indefinite term. The expectations created by this arrangement have no doubt grown over the years, and some argue that they have been abused (Keffeler, 1997, p. 6). It is generally understood that tenure can be terminated only for specific reasons and in accordance with specified procedures. The source of tenure "rights," the relevant institutional documents, contracts or appointment letters, and the prevailing case law in the jurisdiction of the institution are all variables unique to the campus; administrators and board members must carefully fathom these issues with legal counsel before proceeding (*Law and Higher Education*, 1998). Certainly one of the many questions will concentrate on the locus of tenure. Is the expectation of tenure tied to a program or to the institution? The degree to which tenure may be program specific is critical to an overall evaluation of the implementation of program prioritization.

My consulting travels have taken me to campuses where nonteaching faculty, including student union managers and residence hall directors, have been granted tenure. The occasion of program prioritization may permit cleaning up such inconsistent and unwarranted practices.

In addition to discontinuance, reduction, and tenure policies well in place, the campus will want to revise existing policies or create new ones suggested through the program prioritization process. How many faculty and staff constitute a "department" has been mentioned. Does the prioritization analysis suggest any rethinking about allocation of faculty loads? Have student credit hours been applied appropriately to reflect differing levels of instruction: lower division, upper division, graduate and professional 1, graduate and professional 2, and so forth? Has the institution lost control, through adherence to specialized accreditation, of the time it takes a student to complete a degree? How institution-wide should the movement toward competency-based education be embraced?

Accreditation

Implementation of program reallocation decisions may also affect one or more of the institution's relationships with accrediting bodies. In addition to the general accreditation conferred by its regional accrediting association, the institution may have been designated by one or more credentialing entities in the state or nation. Certain assumptions may have been made about students of the college or university qualifying for certification or licensure on completion of prescribed graduation requirements. In some instances these arrangements may have historically necessitated agreements or obligations on the part of the institution. As programs change, the campus needs to determine the extent to which it wishes to retain—or indeed continues to be eligible for—specialized accreditation or authorization for licensure and certification.

A typical example involves teacher education. Most four-year colleges in the United States prepare graduates for roles in K–12 education. The responsibility for certifying teachers typically rests with the state's department of public instruction, state board of education, or similar other governmental body. Institutions of higher education are authorized, under varying circumstances, to offer teacher education programs that may lead to certification on graduation. Universities may also be accredited by the state to offer graduate work needed by teachers, K–12 administrators, and other education professionals. It is difficult to generalize about the myriad of these relationships—there are, after all, fifty of them—but it is clear enough that colleges and universities must examine the impact, if any, that program reallocation decisions may have on these arrangements.

Probably no other profession is more bureaucratically dominated than teaching. Some states will insist on adherence to bureaucratic minutiae in the discharge of its responsibilities to enforce professional standards expected of a fledgling teacher. In any given year, a state's legislature will introduce (but hopefully kill) dozens of new requirements leading to more laws and more regulations governing the preparation and retention of teachers, what they teach, and how they should teach it. Faculty in college teacher education programs must operate at the unhappy junction of state department regulations, academic disciplinary concerns, specialized accreditation mandates, if any, as well as institutional imperatives. Keeping it all straight and still turning out good teachers is a challenge.

Occasionally faculty in affected program areas will sound alarms about not making changes in programs because it will adversely affect accreditation. Truth does not usually support these allegations, but they need to be explored. An independent investigation, conducted by the provost to secure firsthand information about the flexibility accompanying specific standards, rules, and regulations, is necessary. Often a campus interpretation of regulations and standards is inaccurate, and a current review may reveal room for waivers or differing interpretations. As an example, some campus faculty will interpret a requirement from the state to cover a topic as meaning that a separate course must be offered, when, in fact, several topics can be adequately covered and the standard met in providing only one course.

Accreditation is obviously important. It plays a strong motivating role in overall institutional planning efforts. "Self-studies for accreditation purposes" is the most regularly occurring institutional planning activity, and accreditation requirements rank second only to the president as a "moving force" behind institutional planning efforts (Dickeson, 1994).

At the same time, higher education accreditation is undergoing significant change. Colleges and universities need to monitor several national developments carefully and choose their positions among competing accreditation issues. Accreditation in the past several decades has meant at least three things. First, regional accrediting bodies were charged with the responsibility of ensuring that institutions (at first secondary schools, then colleges) met minimum standards of quality. Second, through the growth of specialized accrediting agencies and the further development of the regional associations, emphasis was built on improving quality. Finally, accreditation took on a gatekeeper role, certifying to the federal government that institutions were appropriately eligible for receiving federal funds. In the 1990s the reconciliation of these three functions, perhaps never in perfect balance, fell apart (Edgerton, 1997). What emerged from the ashes is the new Council for Higher Education Accreditation (CHEA) with a new organizational structure and a tightened focus. Although it is premature to determine what may be the eventual results of CHEA's efforts, it is reasonable to recommend that institutions look for the following changes:

- Development of more salient national standards for accreditation, but applied regionally or possibly interregionally
- A decided shift toward quantifying student outcomes, as opposed to inputs, laying particular stress on learning outcomes
- Sector-specific standards for institutions of similar type, in addition to basic institutional standards
- An increased emphasis on public accountability

Accreditation in the United States faces challenges entirely reflective of the very changes confronting the institutions that voluntarily submit to it. How to deal with issues of distance learning, nontraditional providers of postsecondary education, and new international dimensions of assessing quality are among the emerging questions (Phipps, Wellman, and Merisotis, 1998).

A final national accreditation issue is simultaneously played out at individual institutions: the proper role for specialized accreditation. Today there are scores of specialized agencies, directly related to hundreds of academic disciplines, that offer specialized accreditation to programs on campuses nationally. Many campuses tout with pride their pedigree of specialized accreditations as a proxy for quality. Yet institutions are recognizing several concomitant issues: most such specialized accreditations are guild-centric and often overemphasize quality inputs that appear self-serving and prove costly; the overlap of periodic self-studies, visits, and institutional responses associated with seeking multiple accreditations causes havoc on campus and begs for greater coordination; and competition within certain disciplines has resulted in rival groups' purporting to represent the same content specialty.

As colleges and universities implement decisions emanating from program prioritization, the relationship between the institution and the accrediting bodies it elects to embrace will have to be kept in mind. Regional accreditation staff are open to questions and calls about standards and interpretation of intended campus actions that might affect continuing accreditation. At the time of program resource reallocation, it may also be wise to weigh the relative costs and benefits of specialized accreditation.

Humane Dimensions of Reallocation

Separating individuals from an organization is never easy, and it is notably stressful in higher education. Program decisions that result in separation of students, faculty, and staff should be handled in as humane a way as possible, befitting the special character of the institution and accomplished with as little damage as practicable to its sense of community. That being said, the difficulty in maintaining morale under circumstances of retrenchment will test the sensitivity, communication skills, and leadership of the very best individuals required to fulfill these unpleasant but necessary duties (Dickeson, 1991).

The experience of campuses that have undergone these tasks is instructive and can be framed in five admonitions.

Focus on Students. The campus should work with students in affected programs on an individual basis. A personalized assessment of unmet program requirements for students in the pipeline is essential. The college should exercise optimum institutional flexibility in permitting substitute courses, independent study, and waivers of program requirements to balance out the degree-completion needs of the student with respectable academic standards. Cooperative arrangements with other colleges to take courses should be considered. It may be necessary to phase out or delay a program discontinuance by one or more terms to accommodate students' course, research, or other degree requirements. This delay may necessitate the retention of faculty on term contracts for this purpose.

In some instances facilitating the transfer of students to other programs on campus or even to other institutions can be helpful. Making contacts with relevant programs at other campuses, waiving transcript fees, and cutting through bureaucratic red tape should be minimal expectations. At one campus I was retained to facilitate the transfer of fine arts majors from a program being closed down for severe financial exigencies. I found professionally sympathetic and willing participants at dozens of other colleges and universities around the country, and all students were eventually placed in such programs. Focusing on students is not only the hallmark of a student-centered campus; it also communicates to all campus participants the primacy of the institution's mission.

Exhaust Less Drastic Means. If at all possible, the institution should undertake a combination of personnel actions designed to eliminate, or at least minimize, the impact of outright reductions in force. Time-honored practices include the following:

- Short-term sabbaticals, leaves without pay, leaves with partial pay, and/or furloughs, in which payrolls can be reduced while maintaining employment relationships
- Work-sharing plans that reduce hours per week but retain work arrangements
- Capture and reallocation of positions due to attrition
- Early retirement programs
- Negotiated exchanges of tenure for term contracts
- Tenure buyouts and severance packages.

Facilitate Alternative Employment. The institution may accept the obligation to find alternative employment for displaced employees in other departments. Some faculty may be willing, if qualified, to accept available positions in administrative jobs. With a reasonable retraining or retooling program—at institutional cost—faculty may become eligible to fill teaching positions in higher-demand programs. And outplacement services should be made available to support faculty applications to positions at other institutions. The myriad professional contacts that a campus community enjoys across the country should be harnessed in efforts to secure employment information for affected faculty. If the campus is part of a multiple-campus system, transfer opportunities should be honored at sister institutions.

Establish Redeployment Options. Affected faculty should be given priority in bidding for positions that become available (all relevant job specifications being equal) in a reasonable period of time. Recall opportunities, should the program again become available, should be offered.

Provide Counseling Services. In addition to career counseling services (interview skill development, resumé updating, office support services, access to job databases), reduced faculty may require personal and family counseling. Remember that faculty positions eliminated due to program reduction (institutional exigency) are not typical dismissals for cause (disciplinary problems). The faculty member has done nothing wrong. Faculty breadwinners, however, trying to explain to the family that they are now out of work, will have great difficulty in communicating to loved ones that it was the position, not the person, that was cut. Convincing the family that one has not failed, that "program prioritization resulted in reallocation of scarce resources," just does not do it. Professional help often is needed to work through very painful times, and the decent institution will provide it, free of charge.

Despite the best intentions of caring people, a reduction in force can impose psychic damage that is deleterious to a college community and may take years to heal.

Maintenance of the Database for the Future

Assembling the storehouse of information required to justify the decisions about program prioritization is a prodigious task. Most self-studies collect dust on shelves and are no longer accessed. It is strongly recommended that *this* database, by contrast, be maintained for future uses. The external demands for accountability and the internal impetus to allocate resources meaningfully are not likely to abate. Programs are dynamic. The demand, quality, cost, and opportunities associated with them change.

Keeping information current and updating formats tied to the program criteria will benefit the institution in numerous ways. All campuses are required to submit to an increasing number of reports and studies for funding, accreditation, or public accountability reasons. The technological transformation of information gathering and retrieval now permits on-line quality review. Information and leadership are becoming more distributed. Planning is surely to become more ongoing and less episodic. Future decisions can be better planned, and anticipation of future needs, issues, and impacts can be better documented.

By maintaining the database and sharing with other higher education institutions, the postsecondary community can communicate with each other more readily the useful information about programs required for benchmarking and internal improvement initiatives.

Colleges and universities will have to communicate their needs effectively if they are to obtain necessary support. Criteria about the programs essential to the academy—captured, formatted, retained, and updated in the institution's database—can provide valuable, useful information that both internal and external publics can understand.

Chapter Nine

Achieving Strategic Balance

The test of a first-rate intelligence is the ability to
hold two opposed ideas in mind at the same time
and still retain the ability to function.
                                                —*F. Scott Fitzgerald*

Academic program prioritization may be viewed in a systematic
way. Borrowing from the theoretical model of Kurt Lewin's (1969)
force field analysis and applying it to what we know about higher
education, we can craft a model depicting how colleges and universities arrive at equilibrium.

Equilibrium

Figure 9.1 represents the phenomenon known to every college
president: higher education institutions operate at the confluence
of multiple pressures. Environmental conditions and pressures are
shown as external driving forces, represented by the arrows pushing toward the institution. At the same time internal restraining
forces impinge on the institution and represent conditions and
pressures that keep the institution from moving toward a higher degree of responsiveness to external forces. A force field can be made
up of pressures of varying intensity. A college or university stabilizes
its behavior where the forces pushing for change are equal to the
forces resisting change. Lewin called the result of this dynamic balance of forces the "quasi-stationary equilibrium."

**Figure 9.1. Academic Program Prioritization:
A Force Field Analysis.**

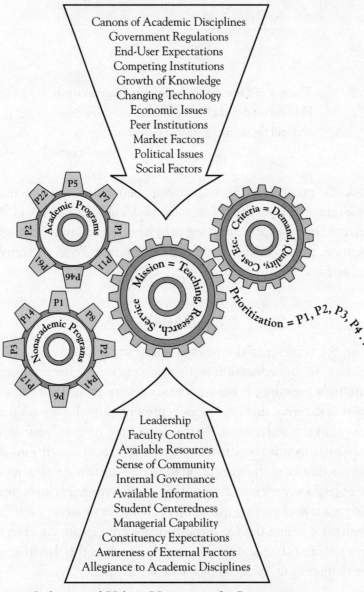

EXTERNAL FORCES
Education Communicators and Socializers

Canons of Academic Disciplines
Government Regulations
End-User Expectations
Competing Institutions
Growth of Knowledge
Changing Technology
Economic Issues
Peer Institutions
Market Factors
Political Issues
Social Factors

Academic Programs

Mission = Teaching, Research, Service

Exc. Criteria = Demand, Quality, Cost

Prioritization = P1, P2, P3, P4...

Nonacademic Programs

Leadership
Faculty Control
Available Resources
Sense of Community
Internal Governance
Available Information
Student Centeredness
Managerial Capability
Constituency Expectations
Awareness of External Factors
Allegiance to Academic Disciplines

Culture and Values Unique to the Institution
INTERNAL FORCES

In this example, the equilibrium represents a more or less open field wherein the institution acts at its existing level because of a balance between external and internal forces. Change can occur only if the forces are modified so that the system can move to and stabilize itself at a different level, where driving and restraining forces are again equal. The equilibrium can be changed by modifying the direction of one or more of the forces. The depiction of the academic program prioritization process represents one such tool for inducing change and, as with all other collegiate processes, operates in the center domain, where the relative effects of forces are played out.

I suggest the following external and internal forces at work; the reader no doubt will be able to supply others equally powerful.

External Forces

Education communicators and socializers: Sources of information about education and its communicated tendencies and expectations

Government regulations: Federal, state, and local administrative regulations that affect the operation of the institution

Canons of academic disciplines: Behaviors and standards of practice for the construction, articulation, and dissemination of an academic content discipline

Political issues: Degree to which forces of the polities affecting the institution, including individuals, aggregating organizations, and elites, ebb and flow in the waters of higher education

Market factors: Extent that market forces, including demographics, awareness levels, price sensitivity, trade, and traffic, manifest demand for higher education programs

Economic issues: Relative state of the economy, particularly regarding those components relevant to higher education, such as disposable income, rate of inflation, degree of unemployment, and perceived value of potential earning capacity

Growth of knowledge: Extent, range, and depth of the geo-
metric growth of the fund of knowledge

Social factors: Expectations from society and its subcultures
that higher education is to be a social institution that both
reflects societal imperatives and changes them

Changing technology: Unparalleled accelerated pace of
change in the development and application of technologies
affecting learning

Competing institutions: Behaviors of other institutions (a
local college, a corporate university, a virtual university)
with powers to displace resources or customers needed by
the institution

Peer institutions: Behaviors of other institutions that the
institution acknowledges as comparator or
aspirational peers

End-user expectations: Expectations of those who use the
institution's "products": employers, research funders, graduate and professional programs, economic development communities, patrons

Internal Forces

Culture and values unique to the institution: The sum total of
ways of behaving that are transmitted from one academic
generation to another at the institution

Constituency expectations: Real and perceived demands
made on the institution by its multiple constituencies:
students, faculty, classified staff, professional staff, alumni,
parents, donors, and others

Allegiance to academic discipline: Extent to which members
of the professorate obey canons of academic disciplines

Student centeredness: Extent to which the needs and expectations of students are measured, understood, and fulfilled at
the institution

Available resources: Availability of money, people, space, equipment, time, and other resources necessary to facilitate the work of the institution

Faculty control: Internal role of faculty, as against other constituencies, in the policy development, authority structures, and other control dimensions of managing the institution

Awareness of external factors: Degree to which the institution perceives the relative impact of any of the external forces

Available information: Extent, depth, and quality of information available to and accessed by the institution in informing its decisions

Internal governance: Degree of involvement by stakeholders in decision making

Managerial capability: Measure of relative expertise in managing the functions of the institution

Leadership: Quality and stability of institutional leadership, directed toward balancing the needs of followers with attainment of mission

Sense of community: Shared belief by members of the institution that they are part of a community

Unique Institutions

Even a moment's reflection on the complex elements of this system will reveal why it is impossible to prescribe any single remedy to the ills confronting a single college or university. The unique impact of one or more external forces and the corresponding reactions from internal forces affirms the conclusion that no two institutions behave alike. How a single college or university will see these elements and coalesce them with what admixture and in what crucible will vary. And so will the results. But as is the case with all other organizations, the results will or will not pass the pragmatic tests of survival.

These forces, internal or external, are as conflictive inherently as they are with each other. What is a "negative" economic factor to some (like high unemployment) historically benefits some college enrollments and hampers others. Social factors are always in conflict, and how the institution accommodates some and ignores others reveals much about its shared values. All the education communicators and socializers in the world cannot penetrate an institution whose awareness radar is on the fritz. Market factors are fickle. How does an institution respond to these realities and at the same time preserve its sense of stability? Forces can also combine with each other: the growth of knowledge, coupled with technological advancements in distance learning, linked with nontraditional virtual universities unfettered by either football teams or faculty senates, can constitute genuine threats—or opportunities.

Not all forces operate unidimensionally. Countervailing forces surface. A major university, for example, exerts its own political influence, affects the economy of its community and state, and makes deposits in as well as withdrawals from the fund of knowledge.

Amid the collision of at least these forces (and no doubt others) academic program prioritization takes place. As Figure 9.1 depicts, programs, unencumbered by analysis in the past but now perceived as needlessly gobbling scarce resources, are measured against the reaffirmed mission and the relevant criteria. Prioritization results, and, with courage, necessary reallocation follows.

It has been said that many collegiate institutions are in the process of achieving transformation. What is shed from the past and what is donned for the future will spell out the success of that process. It is hoped that those who are calling for transformation as well as those who are engulfed in it will see the process in its larger context. What is occurring can be characterized as achieving a new equilibrium for the institution.

Strategic Balance

We tend to conceive of equilibrium in a personal way as keeping one's balance. And so it is with colleges and universities. Thus we come to the conclusion, the end result of this complex and critical prioritization and reallocation process: the achievement of strategic balance. Balance can be defined as "bringing into proper proportion," and such is the nature of the ultimate task of institutional leadership. After all the data are collected, the formats analyzed, the governance processes exhausted, the academic tea leaves read and stirred and read again, and the decisions finally made, what does the new institution look like? What challenges can it now surmount that were insurmountable before? What hallmarks of quality now adorn its escutcheon? What new initiatives will it pursue that demonstrate its control of the future? How will it keep its balance?

The experiences of every college and university president I have known mirror my own in one significant way: we have all faced the simultaneous challenge, frustration, and satisfaction that come from trying to strike a proper balance. E. Gordon Gee, now in his fourth presidency, once likened the delicacy and importance of this task to that of a small boy cavorting atop a picket fence.

Achieving a strategic balance has at least the following twelve dimensions.

1. *Balancing functions: Teaching, research, and service.* Probably no other internal academic debate in this century has been more keenly argued than the proper balance among the three legs of higher education's function stool. The teaching, research, and service functions reflect, to the extents they are performed on a single campus, the relative values allocated to each and the assigned weight of the constituencies each purports to serve. A corollary issue is the effort that should be expended toward undergraduate versus graduate programs. The most recent of the Carnegie Foundation reports restates the familiar points and declares that the nation's research institutions need to reinvent undergraduate education, in part by expanding more student-directed research (*Reinventing Undergraduate Education*, 1998). The overwhelming number of colleges and universities are not research institutions, and the indictment of imbalance is being leveled against all who would

shortchange the student learner at the expense of a misdirected reward system. For each institution, a synthesis of artful poise among its stated functions will be required.

2. *Balancing purposes.* In Chapter Three, several purposes common to colleges and universities were enumerated, among them preparing students for careers, teaching how to think, and liberating the individual. Not all purposes apparently hold equal sway. The reconciliation of relative value among these purposeful aims for a given institution requires care and attention.

3. *Managing fiscal expectations.* It is argued that colleges and universities generally fail a coherence test. To the extent that planning is embraced on a campus, it is somehow disengaged from budgeting. And budgeting is disconnected from accountability. The expectations of all three (planning, budgeting and accountability)— that scarce resources will be responsibly allocated, measured, and reported—ought to prompt the leadership to secure better linkage among these important management tools.

4. *Achieving congruence.* Strategic goals and priorities of the institution, once assigned, need resources to sustain them. Resources cannot be squandered on past goals and priorities or for an institution that no longer exists. Achieving congruence between ends and means marks the well-balanced institution.

5. *Accomplishing affordability and accessibility.* The public has clearly communicated two perceived truths: higher education is necessary, but higher education is too expensive. As institutions try to justify charging loftier tuition prices by making deeper discounts, the stretch between responsible stewardship of resources and providing access to students who deserve higher education becomes more stressful. This freshman "tuition discount rate" at private colleges and universities that are desperate to buy some students by playing Robin Hood with other students' dollars has reached a new high: a mean of 30.14 percent in fall 1997 (*National Enrollment Management Survey Results*, 1998). All but a handful of elite institutions are in danger of pricing themselves out of the market and

simultaneously inviting governmental price controls. Both dangers are unacceptable.

6. *Balancing stability and flexibility*. All good programs require capable and motivated faculty to sustain them. Four elements of faculty mobilization beg for proper balance: full time versus part time, and tenure or tenure track versus contract. Institutional personnel practices are in significant transition. Some colleges, eager to redress imbalances in full-time, tenured-up inflexibility of the past, swing the pendulum toward a new imbalance of part-time, contract-based flexibility of the future. But it is a college or university situated at the fulcrum. Wisdom surely necessitates a long-term view of what matters most in the academic life and scholarly vitality of the institution. Knowing and achieving the required investment in long-range permanent as against the expeditious, short-term temporary will characterize the essence of the institution's commitment to any of its purposes.

7. *Harmonizing institutional interest and public interest*. All institutions, even those relatively independent of public funding, have public obligations. The public interest is more than the sum of special interests. The public confers certain powers on higher education institutions: to credential its graduates, its creative works, and its program offerings. These powers must be met with corresponding obligations to ensure the public of academic currency, quality, and legitimacy. When institutions do not define success indicators that work, the public will create its own.

8. *Respecting tradition and readying for the future*. What to keep, what to abandon; what to embrace, what to champion? The artful balance of legacy and promise will challenge the best leaders of the best institutions.

9. *Reconciling competing expectations*. Colleges and universities exist for many reasons, and people come to them with varying expectations. The patron expects a performing arts production of excellence. The legislator demands that credits transfer from another institution. The parents who have borrowed on their retirement

funds to afford tuition and fees for their children expect value and excellence. The donor needs to be thanked seven times. The grant agency questions indirect rates. And the queue lengthens. Successful institutions focus on doing *some* things especially well for *some* people.

10. *Integrating liberal arts and career preparation.* Colleges and universities must strike a healthy balance between career preparation and liberal arts programs. The traditional either-or arguments are decreasingly persuasive; the future that students will confront demands both.

11. *Planning top down and bottom up.* Hierarchies are collapsing. Authoritarian approaches do not work. Participation is essential. Support for decisions is predicated on ownership of decision making. Asking persons closest to the action to advance their best judgments about programs, and within the framework that makes sense for the institution as a whole, heightens the probability that the results will achieve proper balance.

12. *Delineating authority and responsibility.* Campus practice in the recent past has probably operated to mislead people into the belief that authority and responsibility could somehow be decoupled. They cannot (MacTaggart and others, 1998). A proper synthesis starts with governing boards and moves throughout the organization: it is patently unfair, administratively unsound, and ethically bankrupt to expect one to assume responsibility for a program, a department, a school, or a university without concomitant authority.

Conclusion

Among the final steps toward institutional transformation, leaders will want to consolidate the improvements made, track and report on successes to stakeholders, and continue to inspire still more change. With each iteration, planning effectively can increase credibility to change systems, structures, and policies that do not fit the reaffirmed mission of the institution. Focusing on people who are implementers, rewarding practices and behaviors that confirm the vision, and reinvigorating the prioritization process with new challenges and themes can serve to institutionalize new approaches that lead to new successes.

The ultimate goal is to place the institution in the best possible position, ready and capable of responding effectively to new contingencies at the same time that it goes about shaping its future.

The challenges confronting American higher education are not irresolvable. It *is* possible to identify and eliminate unnecessary duplication of programs and resource-draining deadwood. It *is* possible to reinvest precious resources from lower-priority to higher-priority programs. It *is* possible to plan, define, and measure educational outcomes worthy of continued and expanded public support. It *is* possible that the entire institution can become more than the sum of its self-interests. And above all, it *is* possible to harness better the enormous power of higher education to support the largest and most noble aims of a free society.

Resource A: Outsourcing Practices in Higher Education

I. Most Common Reasons Cited for Outsourcing

    1. Reduces costs
    2. Ensures accountable results
    3. Upgrades program quality
    4. Increases customer satisfaction
    5. Gains access to special expertise

II. Most Common Outsourced Programs and Services

    1. Admissions management
    2. Bookstore management
    3. Campus security
    4. Centralized entertainment booking and contracting
    5. Conference center management
    6. Continuing education centers
    7. Counseling, testing, and psychiatric services
    8. Custodial and housekeeping services
    9. Day care centers
    10. Dining and food services
    11. Facilities management
    12. Human resources: Payroll, including benefits administration
    13. Human resources: Temporary services, training functions
    14. Legal services
    15. Motor pool operations
    16. Physical plant maintenance

17. Printing and publishing services
18. Remedial education
19. Student financial aid administration
20. Student housing
21. Student health services
22. Technology access and computing services
23. Tuition payment services

III. Questions Campuses Ask in Deciding Whether to Outsource

1. Is the service to be privatized (outsourced) critical to our mission? Is it core? Is it a part of our strategic vision for the institution?
2. Can it be outsourced for an increase in revenue or for a savings in costs?
3. Can quality of service levels be maintained or improved?
4. Are hard dollars actually going to be generated, which can then be reallocated? Can a discrete sum of money actually be quantified?
5. Have our labor costs, due to the institutional wage scale and increases in benefits, outpaced the financial viability of the institution?
6. Are other institutional policies, such as personnel and accounting, forcing costs higher than the benefits derived from doing it in-house?
7. What will be the impact on employee morale?
8. Will we still maintain an adequate degree of control?
9. What are future costs if we do not make the decision to outsource?
10. Can we keep the service in-house and save money through restructuring or reengineering instead of outsourcing?
11. What other factors besides the financial ones are going to influence our decision:
    a. Difficult personnel problems?
    b. Intractable management issues?

    c. Governing board pressures?

    d. Fear of not staying competitive?

    e. Liability or legal exposure issues?

12. How will economies that result from the outsourcing be tracked and accounted for?

13. Are any services currently provided in the traditional operation unique or unlikely to be duplicated by the outsource?

14. Is there high employee turnover?

15. Is employee training or keeping up with needed changes a factor?

16. What external factors affect our ability to stay on top of this area? Rapidly changing technology? Changing customer expectations? High degree of government regulation?

17. What is our in-house service record? Are internal and external customer expectations being met?

18. Is the service on an upward or a downward trend?

19. Are equipment costs an issue? Is it practicable that we can afford the new equipment necessary to run the current operation in a more streamlined and efficient way?

20. Have internal or externally driven funding cuts reduced staff levels below the critical mass necessary to run the operation well? Or will they in the near future?

Resource B: Sample Process Agenda Adopted by a Land Grant University

Stage 1: Preparation Stage

Defining a program at the university. Examples:

The Biology Department is responsible for eleven programs:

Biology—B.S. general biology major

Biology—B.S. botany emphasis

Biology—B.S. zoology emphasis

Biology—baccalaureate minor

Biology—General education component

Biology—Service courses to other undergraduate programs

Biology—M.S. botany

Biology—M.S. zoology

Biology—Ph.D., multiple concentrations

Biology—Service courses to other graduate and professional programs

Biology—Public service component [special institute]

The Physical Plant is responsible for four programs:

Physical Plant—Maintenance of buildings

Physical Plant—Utilities

Physical Plant—Preventive maintenance

Physical Plant—Assistance with new construction

As there are hundreds of such "programs" at the university, this stage will involve the consultant, working with the provost and the vice presidents to establish the parameters, design the data collection formats, decide on weighting of criteria for future modeling of outcomes, as well as conducting information sessions for the Strategic Planning Committee, the deans and directors, and department heads.

Stage 2: Information-Gathering Stage

Data about programs are generated from three sources:

1. As many data as are readily available centrally, from Institutional Research and other campuswide offices and sources. This is intended to reduce the burden on individual departments.

2. Individual departments are to provide information along the eight chosen criteria (demand, quality, size, productivity, cost, availability of personnel, maturity, and overall justification). Departments are expected to put their best case forward, due to the promise of enrichment. Many of the data are available from existing accreditation reports, self-studies, and planning efforts already under way by some of the deans.

3. Some data are available from national sources that can be accessed by the consultant (for example, national demand data).

Departments forward the information about all of their programs to their respective dean or director, following the standardized report formats.

Stage 3: First Analysis Stage

1. Deans and directors will review the program information for all programs under their jurisdiction, on a comparative basis.

2. Deans and directors publish, campuswide, rankings of all their programs, using the approved criteria and weightings, along the following quintiles:

   Upper 20 percent: Outstanding programs, candidates for enrichment

   Second 20 percent

   Third 20 percent

   Fourth 20 percent

   Lowest 20 percent: Lower-ranked programs, candidates for reduction, consolidation, merger with other programs

3. Deans and directors will also publish recommendations of efficiencies that might be gained by cooperative or collaborative efforts with other units of the university.

4. Deans and directors will conduct hearings on the published recommendations and receive input and suggestions for improving and refining the ratings and recommendations.

5. Deans and directors will forward to the appropriate provost or vice president the revised recommendations.

Stage 4: Second Analysis Stage

1. The provost and vice presidents will review the program information and render independent judgments on a comparative basis for all programs under their respective jurisdictions.

2. The provost and vice presidents will publish, campuswide, rankings of their programs, using the approved criteria and weightings, along the five quintiles identified in Stage 3.

3. The provost and vice presidents will also publish recommendations of efficiencies that might be gained by cooperative and collaborative efforts with other units of the institution.

4. The provost and vice presidents will conduct hearings on the published recommendations and receive input and suggestions for improving and refining the ratings and recommendations.

5. The provost and vice presidents will forward the revised recommendations to the president and the Strategic Planning Committee (SPC).

Stage 5: Final Analysis Stage

1. The president and SPC will review programs and render independent judgments on a comparative basis for all programs of the university. The consultant will also review programs and will render an independent, third-party judgment on a comparative basis for all programs of the university.

2. The president and SPC will publish, campuswide, rankings of all programs, using the approved criteria and weightings, along the quintiles identified in Stage 3.

3. The president and SPC will conduct hearings on the published recommendations and receive input and suggestions for improving and refining the ratings and recommendations.

Stage 6: Integration and Synthesis Stage

1. The president and SPC will integrate and synthesize the results of the program prioritization process with those relevant portions of any task force reports, the past strategic plans and planning efforts reports, and other relevant information available to the president and the SPC.

2. All recommendations from the president and the SPC must conform with the letter and spirit of the board-approved

Statements of Role and Scope, Mission, Vision, Goals, and Values.

3. This synthesized report will constitute the Master Strategic Plan of the University, and will then be forwarded to the board for its approval.

Stage 7: Final Decision Stage

1. The Board of Trustees will review the Master Strategic Plan, and may elect to hold hearings on its own to receive input, secure recommendations for improvement, and obtain endorsements from interested groups.

2. The Board approves the final plan and establishes the implementation schedule, and directs the President, the Provost and Vice Presidents, and the SPC to implement the Plan.

Stage 8: Implementation Stage

1. The consultant works with the President/Provost/Vice Presidents/SPC to reduce the Plan to ranked, achievable, measurable objectives.

2. Objectives of highest priority will be designed to be implemented over the first year and will include major program decisions, relocation, consolidation, reorganization issues, and significant reallocation of resources.

3. Format of objectives:

Outcome	To have merged Programs A, B, and C into a successful coherent new Program, D, by March 15, 199X.
Cost	Net savings to the University of $240,000, one-third of which will be retained by the Dean for reallocation purposes within the College; one-third of which will be retained by the

>Provost for reallocation within the Division; and one-third of which will be retained by the President and the SPC for reallocation across the University.

Responsibility	Provost
Cost Center	Academic Affairs
Measure	Independent academic judgment from panel of three external experts in the field of D, selected by the D Chair, the Dean, and the Provost.

4. Reporting. At least on a quarterly basis, the President and the SPC leadership will report to the Board of Trustees on the progress being made in implementing the Master Strategic Plan. Reports to the public, special executive briefings to state leaders, and special presentations to key legislative committees will be regularly scheduled.

Stage 9: Renewal Stage

1. All data generated in the development of the program prioritization process should be electronically stored and periodically updated for use in maintaining an ongoing database for continuing program analysis purposes.

2. Periodically, Deans/Directors and Provost/Vice Presidents should be required to reevaluate programs and to maintain ongoing quintile rankings.

3. The President will want to maintain relative priority rankings for enrichment as well as possible reduction reasons on an ongoing, dynamic basis.

Resource C: Criteria for Measuring Administrative Programs

I. Suggested Questions for Administrative Units
   1. What are the main objectives of your unit, and how do you measure success in achieving them?
   2. What are the services that your unit provides and to which customers (students, faculty, staff, donors, others)?
   3. List each position in your unit, and briefly describe the responsibilities of each. Include part-time and work-study student hours.
   4. Do you see needs and demands for services that your unit cannot currently meet? If so, what are they, and how do they relate to the university's mission?
   5. How could the university help your unit do its job better?
   6. In what ways does your unit relate to other units of the university, academic and nonacademic? For example, what services do you provide to other units? What services do other units provide to you? On what tasks do you collaborate with other offices?
   7. What skill sets and resources does your unit possess that can be shared with other units at slack times?
   8. Which individuals in your unit are cross-trained and in what areas?
   9. What resources do you need to improve your services to a superior level?
   10. What technologies are available to you to provide your services better? What training do you need to be more effective users of the technology?

11. What one thing do you wish you could do differently to improve your effectiveness but have not had the opportunity, time, or resources to do?

12. How do you review and evaluate your department's yearly performance?

13. Explain how your unit could function with
    a. A 10 percent reduction in staff
    b. A 20 percent reduction in staff
    c. A 30 percent reduction in staff
    d. A 10 percent reduction in nonpersonnel resources
    e. A 20 percent reduction in nonpersonnel resources
    f. A 30 percent reduction in nonpersonnel resources

What would be the consequences or other effects on service delivery in each case?

II. Suggested Questions for Analysis

1. What opportunities exist for greater collaboration and team approaches in the delivery of services?

2. How many "middle managers" do we have? Are there opportunities to reduce middle strata in the organization and expand the span of control?

3. What technological improvements could be made that would result in labor savings?

4. How can a service be more efficiently delivered?

5. What processes do we have that can be streamlined or eliminated to improve service delivery?

6. Restructuring: What efficiencies might be gained by consolidating similar entities?

7. Personnel: Have we "worked around" or "structured around" deadwood and other personnel issues, and is this the time to stop indulging and start confronting them?

8. Outsourcing: Are there other opportunities to outsource non-mission-critical services to private contractors who could do it better, faster, or cheaper?

9. Customer focus: How might our services be structured or delivered to meet the needs of students, faculty, staff, donors, and others better?

Resource D: Case Studies: Excerpts from Implementation Plans

A Private Comprehensive College: Implementation Letter to College Community from the President

Attached are listings by the schools of the outcomes of the just completed reviews of our academic programs. These conclusions are based on a careful review of the self-evaluations done by each program in light of the factors described below. The Board is in agreement with these conclusions.

Our aim is to be nationally recognized as one of the top ten [comprehensive colleges] in the country by the year 2000. That vision, along with our mission statement and a commitment to being candid about both our strengths and our weaknesses, provided the framework for these reviews and evaluations.

The overriding principle which guided the decisions of this process has been the *enhancement of quality in all our academic programs*. It was acknowledged from the beginning that this was not likely to be a cost-saving exercise. Rather, true enhancement of quality will require more, not fewer financial resources. I am cheered by the initial responses of outside funding sources to the initial goals of our strategic and long-range plan, and I believe the opportunities for fundraising to implement the academic program changes will be equally positive. The identification of sources of support becomes an important next step, and our Board is committed to providing leadership toward that end.

Another important principle in this review was our commitment that no student shall be adversely affected by any program decision. If a major is eliminated, then any student currently registered in that major will be given reasonable opportunity to complete the program as it is phased out. In most cases, discontinuance of majors will only affect students entering in the Fall. During the next two weeks, Department Heads will meet with students whose majors are being discontinued to outline program completion options. Meeting times will be posted in Department offices, in the [student union], and in the residence halls.

In addition, all past decisions with respect to the granting of tenure will be honored. Programmatic changes resulting from this review will be a factor in the granting of tenure for the future, effective immediately.

A review of our College catalog and our student recruitment literature quickly reveals that we list more degrees and programs than can be offered with the quality to which we are committed, given our current number of faculty members. It is important that we gain greater focus in our curricular offerings if we are to achieve clarity and credibility in our public image, and if we are to ensure that our programs are of the highest quality and that our faculty effort is not diluted. We must be certain that the courses for any program we advertise are offered frequently enough that a student can complete that degree in a timely manner.

Among the purposes we strove to achieve were: (a) better focus in our degree options and majors in order to avoid dilution of quality and over-extension of faculty effort, and (b) greater clarity in the way our programs are defined so that we can more effectively communicate with prospective students and the general public. One action which emerged across various programs, therefore, was the discontinuance of some of the multiple degree and program options within the separate academic areas. This, we believe, will lead to more clarity of definition and more effective use of our human and financial resources.

A reduction in the number of degrees or standing majors we offer will not necessarily diminish the rich breadth of curricular opportunity our students have, if we take advantage of the student-initiated major for those who wish to pursue individualized programs. On the other hand, we will improve significantly our credibility with the public, our students, and important external agencies if we discontinue those programs which we either do not have the resources to teach with the highest quality, or in which we cannot offer courses frequently enough for the student to complete degree requirements in a timely manner.

We know that we must increase our enrollment over the next few years and steps are being taken in a number of areas to meet that goal. Enrollment and the quality of academic programs are inextricably tied together: academic programs of excellence are the most important factor in a prospective student's college decision; healthy enrollment is necessary to provide support required for programs of excellence. We must resist the urge to add or maintain academic programs just because they might now have or attract in the future a few students. We must focus instead on offering and delivering an exceptional educational experience to students in each program.

Across our country, institutions of higher education are engaged in similar efforts to examine themselves for the purpose of improving all they do. What we are doing is not different from what other good institutions are doing. These revisions in our programs do not involve the kind of radical change that is happening at some other colleges. For some, perhaps, these outcomes offer too little change; for others, probably far too much.

Change, though, is part of [our] tradition and this is one of our greatest strengths. A number of suggestions for new programs that came forward from the faculty during the process merit further consideration and analysis. It is entirely appropriate for the College to entertain the development of new programs at the same time others are being phased out. Through this process, the curriculum and the College are revitalized, much in the manner that has long been [our] tradition. It will be important, though, that we establish a process for review of any proposals to add new programs to include not just the merit of the idea, but also the impact on faculty, financial resources, and existing programs.

Finally, we need to acknowledge that the review of academic programs should take place on a regular, not a one-time basis. Toward that end, I have requested that the Dean of Faculty draft a procedure for scheduled program reviews in the future.

A Private Liberal Arts College: Selected Academic Program Decisions

Philosophy and Religion

Currently, with a full-time faculty of two, this program offers the B.A. in Philosophy and Religion and a minor in Philosophy and Religion, as well as courses in the general education curriculum. In addition, one faculty member in this program is involved with an interdisciplinary major that involves faculty members from several disciplines. While enrollment has been very low in the Philosophy and Religion major, courses in these areas are basic to our general education curriculum, and the interdisciplinary major has generated significant interest and growing enrollments. Therefore, the College will

A. Retain and, if future enrollments justify, enhance the B.A. in the [interdisciplinary] major. One first step toward enhancement should be the development of grant proposals to fund guest speakers for the program.

B. Retain the minor in Philosophy and Religion, as well as the general education courses in these areas.

C. Discontinue the B.A. in Philosophy and Religion.

Psychology

Currently, the Psychology faculty consists of three full-time members and one part-time member. One of the full-time faculty has announced his retirement at the end of the current academic year. The program offers two B.A. degrees in Psychology (Counseling emphasis and Liberal Arts emphasis) and the minor in Psychology, as well as general education courses. The number of course offerings is extensive, with over twenty-four listed in the current catalog. This is undoubtedly more than can be offered with rigor or reasonable frequency, given the current number of faculty members. Even though the number of courses listed is large, there are areas of psychology considered basic to a good program which are either not offered or offered in less depth than desirable.

In addition, there is an interdisciplinary baccalaureate program, the B.A. in Human Studies, offered jointly by several departments.

As an interest among prospective students nationwide, Psychology stands near the top of the list; indeed, we have a large number of inquiries about this program each year. Enrollments of majors have been relatively good at the College, although retention of majors to graduation should be improved. Aspects of our Psychology program have attracted significant criticism from faculty and students in recent years.

Psychology is an area of significant growth potential for the College if the program could be strengthened to attract and retain good students. For these reasons, the College will

A. Retain and enhance the B.A. in Psychology; offer one, unified and strong major, discontinuing the two separate degrees currently offered.

B. Replace the retiring faculty member with a full-time position whose responsibilities and credentials will be defined by the requirements of the unified major. Consider the addition of a fourth faculty member, if future enrollments justify.

C. Retain the minor and the general education courses.

D. Discontinue the B.A. in Human Studies.

Foreign Languages

The faculty of the Foreign Languages program currently consists of two full-time members, supplemented by the visiting faculty, who teach part-time. They currently offer the B.A. with majors in French, Spanish, and Foreign Languages; minors in French, Spanish, and Foreign Languages; as well as courses in two other languages, Chinese and Russian. The Chinese courses supplement a growing interest and expertise in Asian Studies among some of our faculty.

The opportunity to study Foreign Languages is important to our students if, as graduates, they are to participate in the world community. Enrollments in the major, though, have been extremely small. Available national data on student interests indicate little potential for increases in the number of majors in the foreseeable future.

The College will therefore

A. Retain the minors in French and in Spanish

B. Continue the courses in Chinese, French, and Spanish and discontinue the courses in Russian

C. Continue the Foreign Language courses in the general education curriculum

D. Discontinue the B.A. programs in Foreign Languages, French, and Spanish and the minor in Foreign Language

Academic Computing

Academic computing has grown rapidly over the past several years and now includes computer labs, computers in each department, computers on the desks of faculty members who have requested one, additional computers used for instructional purposes in six departments, as well as computers in the library. In addition, many students have their own computers in the residence halls. A new software program is currently being installed to further enable access to the Internet. Future plans include connecting the labs and faculty offices to each other and to the administrative computing system and fully automating the library. Currently the staffing for

Academic Computing consists of .25 faculty released time each semester.

To adequately support the increased demands by all departments, academic computing will be enhanced through support in the following areas:

A. Increased staff or released time to maintain software library, hardware inventory, and hardware in offices and labs, to train faculty and staff, to administer the various networks, and to evaluate and recommend software and hardware for acquisition.

B. Increased funding for supplies, phone costs, new hardware and software, training materials, student staff to monitor the labs.

C. Commitment to hiring new faculty and staff with computer expertise.

Through the program prioritization process, the need to acquire appropriate technology for instructional purposes emerged as a clear priority which will be addressed. To offer academic programs which prepare students for the 21st century, hardware and software are needed in several programs.

A Public University:
Selected Academic Program Decisions

Interdisciplinary Programs

The new policy requirement to assign all faculty to a specific department for administrative, tenure, promotion, leave and budgetary control decisions is approved. Concern has been expressed that the healthy interdisciplinary nature of some programs may be weakened as a result. To guard against this possibility, the following directives are provided to the respective interdisciplinary program coordinators and the dean of the College of Liberal Arts:

A. All interdisciplinary program coordinators shall be provided .25 FTE released time to assure adequate program coordination.

B. Each of the interdisciplinary areas should maintain or develop advisory committees composed of faculty from disciplines other than the offering department.

C. Overall interdisciplinary coordination shall reside with the dean of Liberal Arts.

D. New interdisciplinary programs, as they become established, should be placed in a department with corresponding advisory committees from among participating disciplines.

College of Music

The demand for performance graduates and music educators at all levels will remain relatively stable during the planning period. The demand for masters and doctorally prepared students in performance, theory and composition, pedagogy, and conducting areas will increase, as will the demand for graduates prepared in the practical aspects of business (arts administration, arts management, arts marketing, music merchandising). Consistent with the recommendations of [the specialized accrediting agency], faculty in the College will be expected to increase scholarly activities. This expectation may necessitate a reduction in the commitment to some of the current service programs sponsored by the College.

The College of Music will continue to contribute to the cultural climate of the campus and the surrounding community through maintenance or reduction of a variety of service programs, including recitals, concerts, operas, musicals, festivals, fairs, symposia, classes, workshops, clinics, and guest artist series. The College will maximize public relations and recruiting potentials of its premier performing ensembles as a means of increasing the visibility and enhancing the reputation of the University as a whole.

The College is expected to increase recruitment efforts aimed toward adding 30 graduate students to its population within the next five years. Additional support will be provided by the College to improve instructional and performance facilities, upgrading performance halls and practice facilities structurally, acoustically and aesthetically. The number of degrees will be reduced, per the recommendations of the Provost, to the five baccalaureate, two masters, and two doctoral degrees, operating within the fourteen emphasis areas.

College of Health Sciences

The demand for all programs in the College will remain high over the next five years. The University will continue to be the primary source for the placement of health professionals in the region. The expense of developing the M.S. in Nursing to a full specialized accreditation status is beyond the means of the University at this time. The College will be restructured as described in this plan as of September 1. The dean shall register his plan for all moves and the phase-out of discontinued programs with the Provost. The dean is expected to coordinate this plan with all other affected deans.

Three of the departments in the College will be candidates for designation as "centers of prominence" within the University. The dean will continue to pursue external funding for the Center for Health Education. By December 1, the dean will submit to the Provost a plan, including structure and proposed operation, for the new interdisciplinary clinic.

A Private University:
Selected Academic Program Decisions

Statement of Program Direction

At [this university], the focus is on the future.

Building on its historically stated mission, [we] seek to prepare the educated man or woman to meet the requirements of the future.

Because the University cannot be all things to all people, we necessarily focus our resources—human, fiscal and physical—on the academic programs and services which help fulfill our mission, and only on those programs and services which we do well. Within available resources we must carefully select and assign priorities to those activities and issues with which the University will align itself. By definition, that means we must reject others, perhaps including some in which we are now engaged, and devote their resources to those we choose to sustain because they are the ones central to our mission.

Unique among independent institutions, [this university] prepares for the future by balancing: (a) the tradition, strength and flexibility of the liberal arts and sciences with the excitement, pragmatism and challenge of selected professions and careers; and (b) the traditions of instructional excellence with the professional and institutional obligations to conduct scholarship, creative and public service activities.

To fulfill this direction and to maintain these balances, the University will sustain a strong liberal arts and sciences core, and support a selected number of professional programs which will allow graduates to compete successfully for career opportunities in their respective fields as well as to pursue advanced educational opportunities.

The academic program prioritization process has been completed. The following recommendations necessarily should be seen only within the context of that prioritization. That is to say, any program being recommended for modification, if it were standing on its own, might ordinarily merit continuation at the University. *But relative to the other programs against which it was measured,* it was found to be wanting. And relative to the resources available to mount the program with distinction, it is recommended to be modified.

Engineering

The engineering programs of the University are designed to provide: rigorous professional degree programs which are competitive with similar programs nationally; scientific research centers which balance the need for scholarship, research and professional service among students, faculty and community needs; and service courses and support needed by other programs of the University.

Electrical Engineering enjoys strong national demand (second quintile) and minimal competition among area universities. The programs are seen as relatively stable. The [specialized] accreditation, the quality research and publication track record and the external funding successes all spell out *excellence*. Size and productivity are below average, due to the extent of the facilities and equipment needs, and the depth of the offerings, through the Ph.D. level. It may be that faculty are overextended with such an array. The program is recommended as a candidate for enrichment.

Engineering Management has had minimal success over the past five years. There is scant national demand, and it is hard to justify this B.S. program with the limited faculty resources dedicated to it. Its internal impact is minimal, and despite the argument that the cost of maintaining the program is minimal, it takes away from focusing on the University's strengths. It is to be phased out.

Mechanical Engineering enjoys a strong national demand (second quintile) and an increasing local trend line. There is minimal competition in the area. Faculty research and publications are good to superior. The low size and low productivity of this program area raise questions about its efficacy, but its presence in a well-rounded engineering program is important. There is good community/industry interaction. The program is recommended to be retained; a separate plan setting achievable benchmarks for continuation is required.

Art

The Art Department is trying to mount both the B.A. and the B.F.A. with four concentrations. This represents an academically questionable stretch for the faculty resources available to the program, and requires a large number of adjunct faculty.

National demand is in the top quintile, but local trend line has represented a significant decline, and there is modest competition from area institutions. There is untapped potential in the computer graphics sequence.

Qualitatively, the students are evaluated through a portfolio review, and while there is minimal data about student outcomes, there is good creative output by faculty.

The size of the program ranks it in the fourth quintile; productivity is average across campus.

Internal impact is important, particularly to the elementary education program.

With two of the three permanent faculty members nearing retirement, it is time to establish a specific academic plan for the department which would include

A. Phasing out the B.F.A. program, but retaining the B.A.

B. Focusing the concentrations on two or three specialties only

C. Phasing out the Studio Art minor

D. Establishing new academic relationships with the community, perhaps through stronger ties with the local gallery

From Several Institutions: Selected Administrative Program Decisions

Tenure and Faculty Evaluation

To ensure the continuing validity of tenure, the Academic Dean is directed to implement a post-tenure performance review process. The need for a performance-based pay system is reiterated, which would include three components: base pay, market adjustment, and merit pay, based on performance.

Effective immediately, the College will work toward a limit of 80 percent of the faculty who may be tenured. This is seen as necessary to provide the College with the opportunity to strengthen both the concept and security of tenure as well as the flexibility to manage its affairs in the future. The percentage will be calculated annually on a school-by-school basis.

Student Affairs

The Student Affairs Division will be reorganized by September 1 to improve management effectiveness by realigning positions and titles and reducing the number of units.

A. Health Services, Student Development Services, Student Financial Aid, Student Life and Activities, and Registrar will report to the Vice President for Student Affairs. Particular emphasis will be placed on the orientation, academic advising, and career planning advisement functions, and this emphasis will require cooperation and support from the entire University community.

B. The Counseling and Career Center, the Health Center and the Resources Center functions will be combined into a single unit, resulting in a net savings of 1.0 FTE.

C. Financial Aid, Veterans' Services, and Student Employment will be reorganized into one unit, with a net savings of .5 FTE.

D. The administrative unit for Special Programs and Services will be phased out, resulting in a net savings of 2.0 FTE.

E. The Registrar's Office will reduce staff by .5 FTE.

F. The Office of Foreign Student Services and the Placement Center will be transferred to University Advancement, resulting in a 12.5 reduction in FTE for Student Affairs; simultaneous reorganization will reduce the net FTE increase in University Advancement by 1.0 of the FTE transferred.

G. The Department of Public Security and the Parking Services area will be transferred to Administration Services.

H. Through the consolidation of Food Services and Residence Life, a reduction of 13.0 FTE will be accomplished.

Financial Affairs

The Financial Affairs area, including Accounting, Operations, Procurement, and Warehouse, will be reorganized to promote efficiency, as will the Physical Plant area, including Plant Administration, Transportation and Motor Pool, Landscaping and Grounds, Planning and Construction, and Building Security. Reorganization will result in a net savings of 9.0 FTE positions. Reductions of personnel in the financial operation will create additional vacancies of 5.0 FTE, of which 2.5 FTE will be used to accommodate the requirement of the State Auditor to add an internal auditor and to augment the staff in the Budget Office.

Administrative Consolidation

The goals of the Administrative Consolidation at the College were to

A. Tighten and streamline administrative operations in all four divisions of the College

B. Reduce duplication of effort

C. Focus efforts and resources on essential services that are more consonant with College purposes

D. Maintain or improve service delivery

E. Save $500,000 in administrative costs, which can be reallocated, through the budget process, to higher priorities among College expenditures

The following means were used to achieve the goals of the administrative consolidation program:

A. Restructuring of operations to consolidate units and to reduce the span of control for managers

B. Eliminating unnecessary, duplicative, or lower-priority positions

C. Expanding supervision duties of key managers

D. Using underutilized personnel more effectively

E. Reviewing classified personnel positions to determine if classifications were appropriate to the positions they occupy

F. Downsizing some operations which have grown beyond original intent

G. Merging similar operations and saving both personnel and operating costs

H. Transferring and reassigning individuals to minimize reductions in force

Offices Affected:

Office of the President—Consolidate reporting relationships, abolish one assistant. .5 FTE savings.

Student Affairs—Consolidate operations of sixteen units into eight units, eliminate one Staff Assistant II position, increase fees, reduce two activities advisors from 12-month to 10-month positions, reassign Dr.... to available vacant position. 3.3 FTE savings.

Academic Affairs—Consolidate reporting relationships, reorganize research administration operations, off-load programs to non–General Fund, reduce engineering support services. 3.5 FTE savings.

College Relations—Consolidate Alumni and Development Office operations, abolish position of Assistant Director of Alumni, transfer one development position to the foundation, abolish one clerical position. 2.0 FTE savings.

Administrative Services—Abolish position of Comptroller, transfer Mr.... to auditing, restructure and reduce Police Department, restructure and tighten internal reporting relationships. 7.0 FTE savings.

Total savings: 16.3 FTE, $788,000.

Administrative Technology

Based on the administrative technology review the following actions are being implemented:

A. All departments with on-line accessibility must utilize purchasing and procurement electronic forms. This will reduce the amount of paper in purchase orders and processes, improve services, streamline operations, and secure automatic commitments to the fiscal reporting system. Estimated savings: $56,000 within two years.

B. Personnel Department will begin automating the time entry process, effective with the beginning of the fiscal year. This will reduce the manual reporting process, increase accuracy, and eliminate the need for paper time cards and manual corrections. Estimated savings: $37,500 at end of first year.

C. Benefits Administration will post information on the Intranet exclusively, thus eliminating the need for printing, stocking and distribution of numerous brochures, forms and other paper-based information. Estimated savings: $15,000.

D. Accounts and Controls will begin to automate inter-fund transfers, rather than submit them on paper forms. This will save on paper, error rates, and department delays. Estimated savings: $56,500 at end of third year.

References

American Association of Community Colleges and others. *Institutional Integrity Review Project*. Unpublished report. Washington, D.C.: American Association of State Colleges and Universities. November 15, 1993.

American Perceptions of the Value and Costs of Higher Education. Public opinion survey commissioned by the American Council on Education. Washington, D.C.: KRC Research & Consulting, 1998.

Astin, A. W. *The American Freshmen: National Norms for Fall 1997*. Los Angeles: University of California at Los Angeles Higher Education Research Institute, and American Council on Education, 1998.

Banta, T. W., and others. *Making a Difference: Outcomes of a Decade of Assessment in Higher Education*. San Francisco: Jossey-Bass, 1993.

Banta, T. W., and others. "Performance Funding Comes of Age in Tennessee." *Journal of Higher Education*, 1996, 67(1).

Banta, T. W., Lund, J. P., Black, K. E., and Oblander, F. W. *Assessment in Practice: Putting Principles to Work on College Campuses*. San Francisco: Jossey-Bass, 1996.

Barak, R. J., and Breier, B. E. *Successful Program Review: A Practical Guide to Evaluating Programs in Academic Settings*. San Francisco: Jossey-Bass, 1990.

Barak, R. J., and Sweeney, J. D. "Academic Program Review in Planning, Budgeting and Assessment." In R. J. Barak and L. A. Mets (eds.), *Using Academic Program Review*. New Directions for Institutional Research, no. 86. San Francisco: Jossey-Bass, 1995.

Barnett, L., and Li, Y. "Disability Support Services in Community Colleges." *American Association of Community Colleges Research Briefs*, 1997, 1.

Barron's Profiles of American Colleges. 22nd ed. New York: Barron's Educational Series, 1997.

Bergquist, W. H. *The Four Cultures of the Academy*. San Francisco: Jossey-Bass, 1992.

Bergquist, W. H., and Armstrong, J. L. *Planning Effectively for Educational Quality: An Outcomes-Based Approach for Colleges Committed to Excellence*. San Francisco: Jossey-Bass, 1986.

The Board's Role in Accreditation. Washington, D.C.: Association of Governing Boards, 1982.

Bogue, E. G., and Brown, W. "Performance Incentives for State Colleges: How Tennessee Is Trying to Improve the Return on Its Higher Education Investment." *Harvard Business Review*, 1982, 60(6).

Boyer, E. L. *Scholarship Reconsidered: Priorities of the Professoriate.* Princeton, N.J.: Carnegie Foundation for the Advancement of Teaching, 1990.

Breaking the Social Contract: The Fiscal Crisis in Higher Education. Washington, D.C.: Council for Aid to Education, 1997.

Bridging the Gap Between State Government and Public Higher Education. Washington, D.C.: Association of Governing Boards of Universities and Colleges, 1998.

Burke, J. C., and Serban, A. M. *Performance Funding and Budgeting for Public Higher Education: Current Status and Future Prospects.* Albany, N.Y.: Nelson A. Rockefeller Institute of Government, 1997.

Chait, R. P., Mortimer, K. P., Taylor, B. E., and Wood, M. M. *Trustee Responsibility for Academic Affairs.* Washington, D.C.: Association of Governing Boards, 1985.

Clery, S. B., Lee, J. B., and Knapp, L. G. *Gender Differences in Earnings Among Young Adults Entering the Labor Market.* NCES 98–086. Washington, D.C.: U.S. Department of Education, National Center for Education Statistics, 1998.

Cope, R. *Strategic Planning, Management and Decision-Making.* Higher Education Report, no. 9. Washington, D.C.: ASHE-ERIC, 1981.

Cope, R. "Academic Program Review: A Market Strategy Perspective," *Journal of Marketing for Higher Education*, 1991, 3(2), 63–86.

Davis, J. *College Affordability: A Closer Look at the Crisis.* Washington, D.C.: Sallie Mae Education Institute, 1997.

DeHayes, Jr., D. W., and Lovrinic, J. G. "Activity-Based Costing Model for Assessing Economic Performance." In *Using Performance Indicators to Guide Strategic Decision Making.* New Directions for Institutional Research, no. 82. San Francisco: Jossey-Bass, 1994.

Dickeson, R. C. "Planning for Downsizing." *SYNTHESIS: Law and Policy in Higher Education*, 1991, 3(4), 206–209.

Dickeson, R. C. *National Survey on Planning in Higher Education.* Society for College and University Planning Southeast Update, January, 1994, p.1.

Dickeson, R. C. Unpublished report to Noel Levitz consultants. Jan. 14, 1997.

Dill, D. D. "Effects of Competition on Diverse Institutional Contexts." In M. W. Peterson and others (eds.), *Planning and Management for a Changing Environment: A Handbook on Redesigning Postsecondary Institutions.* San Francisco: Jossey-Bass, 1997.

Dill, D. D. "Focusing Institutional Mission to Provide Coherence and Integration." In M. W. Peterson and others (eds.), *Planning and Management for a Changing Environment: A Handbook on Redesigning Postsecondary Institutions.* San Francisco: Jossey-Bass, 1997.

Dolence, M. G., and Norris, D. M. *Transforming Higher Education: A Vision for Learning in the 21st Century.* Ann Arbor, Mich.: Society for College and University Planning, 1995.

Donald, J. *Improving the Environment for Learning: Academic Leaders Talk About What Works.* San Francisco: Jossey-Bass, 1997.

Doucette, D., and Hughes, B. (eds.). *Assessing Institutional Effectiveness in Community Colleges.* Laguna Hills, Calif.: League for Innovation in the Community College, 1990.

Douglas, B., Shaw, P. G., and Shepko, R. "Seventh Inning Stretch: A Retrospective of the NACUBO Benchmark Program." *Business Officer,* 1997, *31*(6), 29.

Edgerton, R. *Higher Education White Paper.* Unpublished monograph. Philadelphia: Pew Charitable Trusts, 1997.

Enarson, H. L. "Reform and Renewal of Undergraduate Education." In Robert Zemsky (ed.). *Policy Perspectives.* Philadelphia: Pew Higher Education Research Program, Sept. 1990.

Evers, F. T., Rush, J. C., and Berdrow, I. *The Bases of Competence: Skills for Lifelong Learning and Employability.* San Francisco: Jossey-Bass, 1998.

Ewell, P. T. "Identifying Indicators of Curricular Quality." In J. Gaff and others (eds.), *Handbook of the Undergraduate Curriculum: A Comprehensive Guide to Purposes, Structures, Practices and Change.* San Francisco: Jossey-Bass, 1997a.

Ewell, P. T. "Strengthening Assessment for Academic Quality Improvement." In M. W. Peterson and others (eds.), *Planning and Management for a Changing Environment: A Handbook on Redesigning Postsecondary Institutions.* San Francisco: Jossey-Bass, 1997b.

Farmer, D. W., and Napieralski, E. A. "Assessing Learning in Programs." In M. W. Peterson and others (eds.), *Planning and Management for a Changing Environment: A Handbook on Redesigning Postsecondary Institutions.* San Francisco: Jossey-Bass, 1997.

Fink, I. "Adapting Facilities for New Technology and Learners." In M. W. Peterson and others (eds.), *Planning and Management for a Changing Environment: A Handbook on Redesigning Postsecondary Institutions.* San Francisco: Jossey-Bass, 1997.

Finnegan, D. E. "Transforming Faculty Roles." In M. W. Peterson and others (eds.), *Planning and Management for a Changing Environment: A Handbook on Redesigning Postsecondary Institutions.* San Francisco: Jossey-Bass, 1997.

Footlick, J. R. *Truth and Consequences: How Colleges and Universities Meet Public Crises.* Washington, D.C.: ACE/Oryx, 1997.

Footlick, J. R. "The Holy Cow! Story: How the News Media Cover College Costs." *The Presidency: The Magazine for Higher Education Leaders*, 1998, *1*(1), 28.

Gaff, J., and others. *Handbook of the Undergraduate Curriculum: A Comprehensive Guide to Purposes, Structures, Practices and Change*. San Francisco: Jossey-Bass, 1997.

Gappa, J. M., and Leslie, D. W. *The Invisible Faculty: Improving The Status of Part-Timers in Higher Education*. San Francisco: Jossey-Bass, 1993.

Gardner, J. W. *Excellence: Can We Be Equal and Excellent Too?* New York: Harper & Row, 1961.

Giving USA. New York: American Association of Fund-Raising Counsel Trust for Philanthropy, 1998.

Glen, P. *It's Not My Department! How America Can Return to Excellence—Giving and Receiving Quality Service*. New York: Berkley Books, 1992, 157.

Graves, W. H., Henshaw, R. G., Oberlin, J. L., and Parker, A. S. *Infusing Information Technology into the Academic Process*. In M. W. Peterson and others (eds.), *Planning and Management for a Changing Environment: A Handbook on Redesigning Postsecondary Institutions*. San Francisco: Jossey-Bass, 1997.

Hefferlin, JB L. *Dynamics of Academic Reform*. San Francisco: Jossey-Bass, 1969.

Honan, W. H. "The Ivory Tower Under Siege: Everyone Else Downsized; Why Not the Academy?" *New York Times Education Life*, Jan. 4, 1998, p. 33.

Ikenberry, S. O., and Hartle, T. W. *Too Little Knowledge Is a Dangerous Thing: What the Public Thinks and Knows About Paying for College*. Washington, D.C.: American Council on Education, 1998.

Independence, Accreditation, and the Public Interest: Special Report on Accreditation. Washington, D.C.: National Policy Board on Higher Education Institutional Accreditation, 1994.

Ingram, R. T. *Transforming Public Trusteeship*. Washington, D.C.: Association of Governing Boards of Universities and Colleges, 1997.

Keffeler, J. B. "How Faculty Can Break the Impasse on Tenure." *Trusteeship*, 1997, *5*(6), 6.

Keller, G. *Academic Strategy: The Management Revolution in American Higher Education*. Baltimore: Johns Hopkins University Press, 1983. See also Marchese, T. "Academic Strategy: Five Years Later." *AAHE Bulletin*, Feb. 1988, pp. 3–6.

Keller, G. "Examining What Works in Strategic Planning." In M. W. Peterson and others (eds.), *Planning and Management for a Changing Environment: A Handbook on Redesigning Postsecondary Institutions*. San Francisco: Jossey-Bass, 1997.

Knopp, L. "Remedial Education: An Undergraduate Student Profile." *American Council on Education Research Briefs*, 1995, *6*(8).

Law and Higher Education: Issues in 1998. St. Petersburg, Fla.: Stetson University College of Law, 1998.

Lawson, J. C. "Wall Street Is Watching." *Black Issues in Higher Education*, Jun. 27, 1996, p. 18.

Leslie, D. W., and Fretwell, Jr., E. K. *Wise Moves in Hard Times: Creating and Managing Resilient Colleges and Universities*. San Francisco: Jossey-Bass, 1996.

Lewin, K. "Quasi-Stationary Equilibrium." In W. G. Bennis and others (eds.), *The Planning of Change*. Austin, Tex.: Holt, Rinehart and Winston, 1969.

Lovrinic, J. G., DeHayes, Jr., D. W., and Althoff, E. J. "Developing an Economic Model: How One Midwestern University Is Approaching Cost Control." *Business Officer*, 1993, 27(1), 34.

Lundquist, J. "A Complete Transformation: Activity-Based Costing Represents a Business Revolution." *Business Officer*, 1996, 29(12), 31–33.

MacTaggart, T. J., and others. *Seeking Excellence Through Independence: Liberating Colleges and Universities from Excessive Regulation*. San Francisco: Jossey-Bass, 1998.

McCoy, M. "Governing and Administering Change." In S. L. Johnson and S. C. Rush (eds.). *Reinventing the University: Managing and Financing Institutions of Higher Education*. New York: Wiley, 1995.

McGrath, D., and Townsend, B. K. "Strengthening Preparedness of At-Risk Students." In J. Gaff and others (eds.), *Handbook of the Undergraduate Curriculum: A Comprehensive Guide to Purposes, Structures, Practices and Change*. San Francisco: Jossey-Bass, 1997.

Mets, L. A. "Planning Change Through Program Review." In M. W. Peterson and others (eds.), *Planning and Management for a Changing Environment: A Handbook on Redesigning Postsecondary Institutions*. San Francisco: Jossey-Bass, 1997.

Mingle, J. R. "The New Activism of State and System Boards." *Trusteeship*, 1998, 6(1), 34.

Moody's Investors Service. *Higher Education and Other Not-for-Profits Ratings Group: 1996 Annual Review*. New York: Author, 1996.

Mortimer, K. P. *Joint Commission on Accountability Reporting*. Washington, D.C.: American Association of State Colleges and Universities, American Association of Community Colleges, and National Association of State Universities and Land-Grant Colleges, 1995–1997.

National Association of College and University Business Officers (NACUBO). *Benchmarking for Process Improvement in Higher Education*. Washington, D.C.: Author, 1994.

National Enrollment Management Survey Results, Four-Year Institutions, Fall, 1997. Denver: USA Group Noel Levitz National Center for Enrollment Management, 1998.

Neff, C. B. "Planning and Governance." *Journal of Higher Education,* 1971, 42(1), 116.

Neumann, A., and Larson, R. S. "Enhancing the Leadership Factor in Planning." In M. W. Peterson and others (eds.), *Planning and Management for a Changing Environment: A Handbook on Redesigning Postsecondary Institutions.* San Francisco: Jossey-Bass, 1997.

The Official Directory of Graduate Programs. 16th ed. 4 vols. Princeton, N.J.: Educational Testing Service, 1997.

Phipps, R. A., Wellman, J. V., and Merisotis, J. P. *Assuring Quality in Distance Learning: A Preliminary Review.* Washington, D.C.: Council for Higher Education Accreditation, Apr. 1998.

Reaping the Benefits: Defining the Public and Private Value of Going to College. Washington, D.C.: Institute for Higher Education Policy, 1998.

Reinventing Undergraduate Education: A Blueprint for America's Research Universities. Carnegie Foundation for the Advancement of Teaching, 1998.

Returning to Our Roots: The Student Experience. Report of the Kellogg Commission on the Future of State and Land-Grant Universities, 1997.

Shirley, R. C., and Volkwein, J. F. "Establishing Academic Program Priorities." *Journal of Higher Education,* 1978, 49(5), 472–488.

Skolnik, M. L. "How Academic Program Review Can Foster Intellectual Conformity and Stifle Diversity of Thought and Method." *Journal of Higher Education,* 1989, 60, 619–643.

The States and Graduate Education. Task Force on Graduate Education of the Education Commission of the States. Denver: Education Commission of the States, 1975.

Straight Talk About College Costs and Prices. Report of the National Commission on the Cost of Higher Education. Phoenix, Ariz.: Oryx Press, 1998.

Stringer, W. L., Cunningham, A. F., O'Brien, C. T., and Merisotis, J. P. *It's All Relative: The Role of Parents in College Financing and Enrollment.* USA Group Foundation New Agenda Series, vol. 1, no. 1. Indianapolis: USA Group Foundation, 1998.

Trussel, J. M., and Bitner, L. N. "As Easy as ABC: Re-engineering the Cost Accounting System." *Business Officer,* 1996, 29(12), 34–39.

U.S. Department of Education. National Center for Education Statistics. *Current funds expenditures of institutions of higher education in current dollars, by purpose: Fiscal years 1987 through 1995.* Washington, D.C.: Government Printing Office, 1997.

Wilson, R. "Contracts Replace the Tenure Track for a Growing Number of Professors." *Chronicle of Higher Education,* Jun. 12, 1998, p. A12.

Index

Students: program prioritization and, 98,
111; and program quality, 64
Sweeney, J. D., 48

T

Tax-exempt status, 6
Taxonomy of Postsecondary Education
Institutions, 32
Taylor, B. E., 106
Teacher education, and reallocation deci-
sions, 107–108
Teaching-research-service functions,
34–35, 121
Technology, program adaptability to, 65
Tenure and faculty evaluation study,
150–151
Tenure policies, 17; debate on, 105–106;
and program cuts, 106–107
Title IV federal financial programs, 5, 8
Townsend, B. K., 41

Trussel, J. M., 3
Tuition price: and instructional costs, 8;
and "tuition discount rate," 122
Tuition revenues: federal legislation and,
6; growth in, 2

U

Underfunding, program, 17
Uniqueness, institutional, 54–55,
119–120

V

Volkwein, J. F., 53

W

Wellman, J. W., 110
Wilson, R., 106
Wood, M. M., 106